Civilized Assertiveness® for Women

Communication with Backbone ...not Bite

Judith Selee McClure Ph.D.

ALBION STREET PRESS

DENVER

For information, contact
Albion Street Press
2111 East Alameda Avenue
Denver, CO 80209
www.albionstreetpress.com
www.civilizedassertiveness.com

McClure, Judith S.
    Civilized assertiveness for women : communication
with backbone not bite : the manual / Judith Selee
McClure
    p. cm.
    Includes bibliographical references.
    LCCN 2003103943
    ISBN 0-9729664-3-9

    1. Assertiveness in women. 2. Assertiveness
training. 3. Interpersonal communication. I. Title.

    HQ1206.M25 2003   158.2'082
                                 QBI03-200395

Production Management by
Paros Press
1551 Larimer Street, Suite 1301   Denver, CO 80202
303-893-3332   www.parospress.com

BOOK DESIGN BY SCOTT JOHNSON

Printed in the United States of America
1   3   5   7   9   10   8   6   4   2

Table of Contents

Dedicated, in loving memory,
to my mother, Frances VanKirk Selee,
who by her gracious example
taught me civility
and the importance of respect.

And to my brother,
Richardson Selee, aka DB,
who taught me assertiveness
and the importance
of standing up for myself.

Acknowledgments

I am indebted to four special people in my life who have been unfailingly supportive of the concept of civilized assertiveness over the past 15 years: Priscilla Johnson, my son George McClure, Mary Kelly O'Donnell, and Peter Warren. They sent me relevant articles, helped me polish the concept, refine the materials and equally important, were always there with friendship and camaraderie.

My gratitude to Judy Joseph, President of Paros Press, for putting together a great team. Judy's encouragement, competence, and her most civilized and assertive guidance were essential to the process. The professionalism and contributions of Susan Remkus, master wordsmith, of Copyediting Etc., talented indexer Deanna Butler and ever-creative Scott Johnson of Sputnik Design Works, were wonderful gifts.

My warmest thanks to artist Gary LaCroix. His friendship, design skills and delightful, slightly off-center ideas were a tonic to me over the fifteen years and seven editions of the workbooks leading up to this book.

A particular acknowledgment to Val Williams, my partner in teaching civilized assertiveness workshops. Her youthful energy and enthusiasm for the work, her mature, keen observations and insights, and our vigorous tossing back and forth of ideas have been invaluable.

And finally, loving thanks to my husband, Vincent Vappi. While I was writing this book, he provided constant encouragement and tangible support by endlessly proofing copy and by shouldering all the household responsibilities with kindness and good humor. He is my true partner.

"We intend simply to be ourselves.

Not just our little female selves, but our

whole big human selves."

> – Marie Jenney Howe
> Early 20th Century Founder
> of Heterodoxy

What Is Civilized Assertiveness?

Civilized Assertiveness is a new approach to communication designed especially for today's women. It grew out of my experiences teaching thousands of women in hundreds of communication classes over the past twenty years. In that time, I have been impressed, charmed, and inspired by my students, who bring pressing needs and important questions to each seminar.

* "I am the top producer in my office and yet my ideas are often ignored. Should I try to operate more like a man so I will be listened to and taken seriously?"

* "I am a 'people pleaser' and often give in to others just to keep things pleasant. How can I be decent and considerate and yet be forceful enough to get ahead?"

✳︎ "I need to be tougher to succeed in my job but I don't want to be obnoxious. How can I go after what I want without being pushy?"

✳︎ "My husband (kids/friends/relatives) sometimes makes me feel like a doormat. How can I get more respect? Without nagging, how can I get my family to do some of the housework?"

✳︎ "How can I request and get a raise without whining?"

Over the years, I have heard a clear call for a new way to communicate that combines strength with decency. Women want to find a way to stand up for their rights, accomplish their goals, and be taken seriously—without violating the moral codes they have always used to relate to the larger world. They have found that using traditional feminine speech seems to leave them behind at the gates of power. But they have also found that borrowing traditionally masculine speech often produces a backlash.

My research in developmental psychology, psycholinguistics, and male and female communication styles confirmed what my students were experiencing firsthand. **Women's traditional way of speaking puts them at a serious disadvantage.** Using non-assertive speech patterns undermines their competence and status at work and diminishes their influence in relationships. This critical fact led me to pinpoint communication differences that are barriers to women's success. I identified non-assertive speech and ineffective communication styles that set women apart. To counteract these effects, I culled the best of the time-honored assertiveness techniques and developed new ones. The goal was to give women new ways to speak and behave that project strength and confidence.

The reports from women in my seminars about their experiences in the workplace and "what really works" and "what doesn't work" were invaluable in identifying which organizational behaviors of men that women should adopt and which should be modified or discarded altogether. In addition to considering "What is the effective thing to do?" my students also considered "What is the right thing to do?" There has been a remarkable consensus about which behaviors they felt they could in all conscience adopt and which behaviors they could not, because it violated fundamental values. For example, they were comfortable adopting men's style of seeking out constructive criticism, but they rejected using one-upmanship and put-downs as ways to establish authority.

Women don't want to buy into an aggressive style, but on the other hand they don't want to be "patsies." Often, they see-saw between passive and aggressive behavior. They are tired of the whipsaw of giving in and giving way because it seems natural, and then overcorrecting and becoming angry and aggressive because they've given away too much. Women want to become more balanced in their dealings with others. They want insights, techniques, and guidelines that allow them to:

- Get ahead and get promoted
- Say "No"
- Confront undesirable behavior
- Define and maintain personal boundaries
- Set limits with manipulative people
- Be taken seriously
- Take credit for ideas and work
- Express anger appropriately
- Stop being "nicey-nice"
- Stand up to aggressive people
- Ask for what they want without feeling guilty
- Give and accept criticism

■ Negotiate at work and in their personal life
■ Stop apologizing for everything
■ Stand up for their ideas in the face of opposition
■ Have equal relationships with men

Before the 20th century advent of feminism, women questioned whether they deserved equal pay, equal treatment, equal work, equal opportunities, time off for themselves and all the other things men assume are their natural right. As we begin the 21st century, a majority of women have answered that question with a resounding, "YES WE DO!!!" Now the vital question is "What do I say to get it?" We have the conviction—now we need the words.

So Civilized Assertiveness evolved in response to women's needs to speak and behave in ways that will get them more of what they want. Civility and assertiveness are considered together because they are two sides of the same coin. Civility is ethical behavior toward others. Assertiveness is ethical behavior toward ourselves. In the absence of civility, we act primarily out of self-interest. In the absence of assertiveness, we act without self-interest. Neither course is healthy or desirable.

The focus of Civilized Assertiveness is to balance relationships, not control them; to gain esteem from oneself, not approval from others; to possess "power to," not "power over." It is a comprehensive system that flows from four essential communication skills—Listen, Limit, Assert, Negotiate— and rests on three ethical principles—Respect, Mindfulness, and Balance. Civilized Assertiveness combines women's traditional strength of relating to others with their current need to be confident, competent and influential in important issues at work and in life. It gives women a strong, ethical voice—and with voice comes power.

HOW TO USE THIS BOOK

First and foremost, this is a "how to" book. It teaches the reader specific assertive words and phrases that identify her as a self-respecting, competent person who is to be listened to and taken seriously. At the same time, the book identifies non-assertive, powerless speech habits and self-diminishing talk that women need to banish from their vocabulary.

The first five chapters set the stage for later skills, principles and "how to" steps by demonstrating what Civilized Assertiveness is, why women need it, and why assertiveness does not come naturally for many women. These chapters include a questionnaire and a personal Bill of Rights. They speak to the heart and spirit—I urge you to read them before you move on to the skills.

The middle section of the book teaches the ethical principles and communication skills of Civilized Assertiveness. It provides detailed explanations of how these principles and skills work and what they mean through numerous examples and scripts which illustrate the skills in practice. Take the time to absorb these chapters—even read some of the statements out loud—so that you can become more comfortable in using the words and understanding the concepts behind them.

The last chapters center on women in the workplace. There are more scripts that address common dilemmas and illustrate the civilized and assertive way to solve them, as well as descriptions of special problems women encounter in the workplace and how to handle them with grace. The final chapter pulls together the skills, strategies, and "how-to" steps by integrating them with the Ten Commandments of Civilized Assertiveness for work and in life.

SOME SPECIFICS

* All bullet points— ■ squares and * asterisks—describe or list ideas that further your knowledge of a topic.

✳   Boxes in blue highlight or further break down important
     concepts.

✳   Words, phrases, or dialogue in blue text indicate phrases
     important to Civilized Assertiveness. These are words
     that project confidence, competence or authority.

✳   Note pages with blue borders are scattered throughout
     the book for your own thoughts, reactions, and
     suggestions to yourself.

✳   Many dialogues take place in two columns: The left-
     hand column shows the words being said in the
     conversation, while the right-hand column shows the
     meaning behind the words being said or the assertive
     skill being used in those words.

Remember, this book is meant to be used! Make notes,
pause to reflect on the ideas presented here, and take the time
to practice and incorporate them into your daily life, noting
what does and what doesn't work. Come back to sections that
are particularly helpful for dealing with a current situation that
calls for assertiveness. As you reread and practice these new
habits of heart and mind, observe the changes that take place in
your conversations. Healthy communication is fluid and
dynamic—enjoy the new flow of your relationships.

Talking with the Men in Our Lives

I want to establish up front that many of my best friends are men. I like men and strongly believe that women's rights are not strengthened by deprecating men. To the contrary, my goal is to establish new and better ways to talk to each other across all of our human differences—age, race, class, region, religion, ethnicity, job status, and *especially* gender.

There is a common language we can all choose to speak. It is not a matter of learning a new language, it's a matter of shaping and using the nuances of our mother tongue in cooperative rather than competitive ways. It's a matter of sorting through our impulses and training in order to identify and use language that is assertive but not aggressive, and civil but not passive. Learning this language will enable women to build up confidence, power, and influence. It will make our jobs more productive, our relationships more harmonious, and our lives more fun.

I like men, but I don't see them as special—different yes, but not special or wiser or better. I realized from childhood on that my attitude is not universally shared and that many girls and women view boys and men as a special class possessed of uncommon wisdom and talents not available to "mere" women. Later on I began to notice a corollary to this belief: Men's specialness entitles them to deferential treatment, and a "good" woman has a duty to provide it. Most men I know do little to discourage this attitude. They actively seek to reinforce this view, relish the one-upmanship, and cheerfully lap up the flattery. I'm mildly amused by this, because on close inspection every man I've ever known has been a struggling, fallible mortal—just like you and me.

The men in my life have taught me some important and useful "masculine" ways to think, act, and speak. I value these lessons because they have, in many cases, made my life easier and better. By the same token, I have some valuable "feminine" ways to think, act, and speak that would be helpful to men and would make their lives easier and better. And I have tried to show the men in my life many of these things. I have succeeded in some cases, but almost without exception, it has been a very hard sell. I have known that for some reason, unclear to me, girls and women's words were not as respected and did not carry as much weight as those of boys and men. This understanding has puzzled me enormously across the years. I have spent considerable time pondering why it is so.

My research as a behavioral psychologist, combined with my own experiences and the thousands of shared experiences from the plucky women in my workshops, have led me to my basic premise. *The heart of the issue has very little to do with gender and everything to do with power, influence, and respect.* These three threads are inexorably intertwined. Power differences necessarily lead to different influence styles. And the style of those with less power is *ipso facto* viewed as less influential and deserving of less respect—certainly a formidable

double bind for women.

It's hard to overstate the profound male and female differences in the perception of power—what it is (power "over" versus power "to"), why we need it and how we get and maintain it. Unfortunately, a number—but assuredly not all—of women's traditional ways of speaking make them sound powerless, undermine their influence, and reinforce inequalities both blatant and subtle. To overcome damaging stereotypes, we have to come to terms with the fact that historically and currently, women's language is devalued, and our influence and respect along with it. In 16th century England, Queen Elizabeth the First clearly understood that being a woman negatively influenced her treatment, when she reputedly said, "Had I been born crested—not cloven, my lords—you would not have treated me so."

Today, as our lives are more and more ruled by computers, studies have been done to find out how people react to computerized voices, both synthesized and real. Clifford Nass, a professor at Stanford University, found that we apply gender stereotypes even when we are interacting with something that clearly is neither male nor female.[1] Directions from a female voice are perceived as less accurate than those from a male voice (programmed with exactly the same scripts).

"Deepness helps, too. It implies size, height, and authority," according to Nass. "Deeper voices are perceived as more credible." In study after study, Nass found that the female-voiced computers receive lower ratings than male-voiced computers (using exactly the same words). The female voices were consistently rated less informative in teaching and in giving instructions. Even when it came to giving praise, words spoken by a male voice were valued more highly than those spoken by a female voice.

Good grief! There is something particularly odious about having women's words automatically denigrated by a computer!

As we consider our current and age-old barriers to power and influence, there can be no doubt that we urgently need

clear new words that allow us to form new realities. New words to reflect our new thoughts and convictions—chief among them, the conviction that women's ideas, feelings, and utterances have as much value and weight as men's. We need new words to consolidate the progress we have made and preserve and exercise the hard-won freedoms we have gained. Most urgently, we need new words to discuss what constitutes the proper exercise of privilege and power for *all* of us.

> " From early on, women have recognized the need to take back the language, reclaim it or parts of it, get a right to decide about how to speak and be spoken of and to. "
>
> – Robin Lakoff

Many men are addicted to their special privileges and aren't going to give them up easily. And why should they? Our language and treatment of them support their special status and only benefit *them*. Or is this really the case? When we have good ideas, valid experiences, or judgment or opinions to share, who does it benefit when we hide them and keep silent? We owe it to ourselves and the "other"—but not "better"—half to speak up about what we think, feel, and value. We owe it to the men in our personal lives to share our knowledge, ideas, and feelings with them in order to preserve and strengthen our relationships. We owe it to the men in our work lives to speak

up with our best ideas, innovations, and opinions so that collaboratively we will become more productive. We owe it to our communities and the larger world to speak out on practices and policies we know to be destructive, wooden-headed, or inhumane. And doesn't that benefit us all?

Describing today's women, Rosalind Miles, author of *A Women's History of the World*, eloquently states what lies before us:

> At some point in the last thirty years women looked at each other with new awareness and, sighing at all the work still to be done, understood that whatever they were doing to save the world for women had to be done for men and children, too. Only with the understanding that men and women can unite against all that drags us down will we make a stand for our common health and happiness. That is the task ahead, and we must not fail. [2]

NOTES

The Communication Problem

Ruben, Ruben, I've been thinking
What a good world this would be,
If the boys were all transported
Far beyond the Northern Sea.

Rachel, Rachel, I've been thinking
What a fine world this would be,
If the girls were all transported
Far beyond the Northern Sea.

— Childhood chant

Well, there you have it. The merry dance of courtship aside, boys and girls overwhelmingly prefer the company of their own gender. Important research by Eleanor Maccoby of Stanford University shows that the large amount of time we spend with friends and groups of our same gender throughout life crucially influences our development.[3]

She and other leading researchers have shown that early and ongoing gender segregation produces two fundamentally different cultures light years apart in how they handle relationships, exert influence, and deal with power. It helps explain the resistance that women encounter as they enter the workplace (predominantly a male culture) and strive to take their equal place in society.

Starting in preschool (two-and-a-half to five years old), children show a marked preference for being with a playmate of the same gender. When given a choice about who they want to play with, they spend three times longer with a partner of the same gender. By age six-and-a-half, the time they spend with same-gender partners increases eleven-fold. This pattern carries over into middle childhood, and to a large extent into adolescence and adulthood.

This early and ongoing separation of the sexes profoundly influences the behaviors that evolve within each group. In a very real sense, two distinctive cultures emerge. Each culture, male and female, evolves communication habits that best relate to its own gender. As psychologist Jerome Kagan puts it, the two sexes evolve in such a way that they are "sensitive to different aspects of experience and gratified by different profiles of events."

In other words, males and females interpret and react to the same experience quite differently. What further muddies our understanding of gender socialization is the fact that not only do we react to an identical experience differently depending on our gender; we also react differently depending upon the sex of the person with whom we are dealing!

Following are some typical examples of group communication in the two cultures at preschool age.

PRESCHOOL COMMUNICATION

Group 1	Group 2
■ Give information	■ Listen
■ Tell jokes and stories	■ Acknowledge ideas
■ Top another's story	■ Acknowledge feelings
■ Give orders	■ Express agreement
■ Boast	■ Pause to let others
■ Refuse to comply	into conversation
■ Interrupt	■ Compliment

A friend of mine tells a story that delightfully illustrates these differences. Her grade school twins, a son and daughter, played regularly with neighbors of about the same age. They all loved "kiddy" monopoly so much that she had gotten two boards; the girls played with one, the boys with the other. The boys often disputed whose turn it was, argued over the rules, and were sometimes devious in their tactics to corner the market on one color in order to double and triple the rents. The crowing when one of them won was deafening. The girls generally played quietly in their corner, chattering between turns and getting up occasionally to tend to their dolls or pet the cat. There was occasional conflict but it was usually patched up quickly. Finally, the girls evolved their own game, which they really loved: They took turns buying properties that were side by side so they could be neighbors.

In Margaret Atwood's novel, *Cat's Eye,* a girl of ten describes these pervasive differences between the groups of boys and groups of girls:

> The girls stand in the schoolyard or up on top
> of the hill, in small clumps, whispering. These
> clumps of whispering girls ... have to do with boys,

with the separateness of boys. Each cluster of girls excludes some other girls, but all boys. The boys exclude us too, but their exclusion is active, they make a point of it. We don't need to.

Boys are not the same. For example, they don't take baths as often as they're expected to. Their clothing is khaki, or navy-blue or gray or forest green, colors that don't show the dirt as much. All of this has a military feel to it. Boys pride themselves on their drab clothing, their drooping socks, their smeared and inky skin: dirt, for them, is almost as good as wounds. They work at acting like boys. They call each other by their last names, draw attention to any extra departures from cleanliness. "Hey, Robertson! Wipe off the snot!" "Who farted?" They punch one another on the arm, saying, "Got you!" "Got you back!" *There always seems to be more of them in the room than there actually are.* (Italics mine.)[4]

Why this gender segregation develops in the first place is not well understood. One obvious explanation is that the rough-and-tumble play style of most little boys is offensive to most little girls. Those who do like it are dubbed "tomboys." A less obvious reason has to do with the very different ways in which boys and girls choose to influence others. The most critical time in the development of a child's sense of competence is the age from three to five, as they more and more try to exert influence on the behavior of other children. Little boys attempt to influence others through direct commands (sometime backed up with force), whereas little girls try to influence almost exclusively with polite suggestions. Their approach works with other girls and adults, but is largely ignored by little boys. So girls learn early that they have little influence on male behavior.

Lest you think that I'm trying to paint a picture of all young girls as sweetness and light, let me assure you I'm not.

Way back when, I taught pre-school for several years at the John F. Kennedy Child Development Center at the University of Colorado Medical Center. I certainly had some contentious, combative, and mean-spirited little girls, just as I had some sensitive, quiet, and non-aggressive little boys. But they were a small minority. The point is that while these characteristics are true of some, they aren't true of most. The developmental studies consistently show preschool

> Any time I'm discussing male/female differences, I'm talking about group tendencies: what most boys/men and what most girls/women do most often. When you read "boys/men or girls/women do so and so," please think parenthetically—"most boys/some girls and most girls/some boys."

and grade-school girls groups demonstrate relatively benign, non-aggressive behavior and speech. And when the research looks at physical and overt aggression, boys win the contest hands down. Since many typical gender behaviors and speech patterns are established at quite a young age, this has significant influence on typical adult behavior and speech.

But the picture gets a good deal cloudier when we consider pre-teens and teens. Recently, there have been a number of academic studies, as well as popular non-fiction books, looking at the issue of bullying. There is a new take on girls' "relational aggression," which is seen as a quieter, but powerful form of bullying. While it occurs at all ages, it reaches its peak in the pre-teen and teen years.

Ah—the teens, and the merry dance begins! As psychiatrist Karl Menninger so beautifully put it, adolescents "have pimples on their subconscious." Hormones pouring into young bodies add to the confusion of deciding who they are and what they want to be. While boys are learning to imitate the men they see in their lives and in the media, the girls are learning to imitate the women they see in their lives and in the media—and

with an even more wildly diverse and contradictory set of rules and role models! During this developmentally challenging time, girls are trying to reconcile conflicting messages about behavior and feelings. They have been told "go along to get along" and "ladies don't hit or shout" when conflicts arise. These rules, while intended to encourage civility, can bewilder and may inadvertently end up squelching girls' ability to deal with conflict directly.

Generally and broadly speaking, we do maintain some aspects of our separate gender cultures throughout our lives. But it is at work (with 46% of women currently in the workplace) and in our adult relationships with our significant others that we finally meld with each other. Now, the big question: What happens when individuals from these two still somewhat alien cultures attempt to interact with one another on a regular basis?

The same problem that preschool girls have with influence shows up later, when adults of the same gender are talking to each other. Women continue to be quite successful in influencing each other, but men are not nearly as capable of doing so.

COMMON TRAITS OF MEN'S SPEECH

Voices are louder and they talk more in public.

Decision-making is quicker, but less complex.

Topics introduced more likely to be discussed.

In joint problem-solving, men do more initiating, directing, and interrupting.

Both genders listen more attentively to men.

COMMON TRAITS OF WOMEN'S SPEECH

Adopt some male speech styles: raise voice, interrupt, and become more assertive.

Give "silent applause" to men: smile, agree, nod affirmatively, and gaze more at the speaker.

Generally adapt to pace of interaction set by men, but uncomfortable about the lack of control.

Frequently allow themselves to be interrupted, leading others to ignore, condescend, or steamroll them.

Decision-making is more complex, takes longer and is more inclusive.

The net result of these differences in style is—surprise!—that men exert more influence and gain more power. Can there be any doubt that the central task for today's women is to learn new language habits that increase their influence and power and allow them to establish equal relationships with the men in their lives?

At a time in which gender roles have blurred in unprecedented ways and new opportunities have opened for women and men alike, our American culture remains accustomed to seeing men actively assert themselves—and seek the limelight. At the same time, we expect women to be non-assertive and to direct the limelight elsewhere when it would benefit them to step into it.

Without a doubt, we need new ways of speaking if we are to succeed in places where male behavior is the norm—i.e., most workplaces. We do not have to copy the men chapter and verse, but we do need to go along with and accept enough of the standard operating procedures to function efficiently. This is a fine

line. We will need to retain and refine some of our most effective techniques, such as inclusive decision-making and active listening, and to discard or modify those that sabotage our status and influence, such as subservient speech and not taking credit for our words and ideas.

Today, each gender is moving toward equal participation in many arenas. The context of speech has changed dramatically. Women are earning more than ever, especially if they hold a college degree. Growing numbers of each gender participate actively in the traditional behaviors of the other gender. Gender divisions are by no means gone, but they're going, going.

And yet...

I can still walk into a seminar of 20 successful female managers and hear from more than half of them that they can't get their husbands to share the household chores. I can address a roomful of female workers who excel in their jobs and the majority of them complain that the choice assignments are still going to male colleagues or that they aren't getting the pay increases and promotions that their work merits.

A woman's traditional language habits diminish her. We expect to hear a man take credit, blow his own horn, and insist that his views be heard. But we are not surprised when a woman is self-effacing, apologetic, and easily gives way. A major finding by Dr. Robin Lakoff at UCLA is that what is considered "women's speech" is actually "subordinate speech."

When speech is laced explicitly or implicitly with "Yes sir," "No sir," "If you please, sir," "Should I?" "I would be happy to..." "May I?" "Would it be all right if I...?" the language of subordination is being spoken. We are witnessing a communication approach in which the chief goals are placating, expressing deference, and making peace—not gleaning credit or building influence. We are hearing the language of the powerless.

The issue isn't gender, the issue is POWER. The noted linguist, Suzette Elgin, has researched and written on this topic for the last twenty five years. She reports that the rules of speech are

not different for women; they are different for those with less power. Subordinate, subservient speech is used consistently by employees in low-status jobs such as child care workers, porters, waiters, and janitors. It is used by men as well as women when they are temporarily in a subordinate position and speaking with another person clearly in a position of power and authority. For example, men frequently use subservient speech when being questioned by a police officer, cross-examined by a lawyer, or examined by a doctor. And on the flip side, if the one in the dominant position—the police officer, the lawyer, the doctor—is a woman, she uses fewer subordinate/feminine speech patterns.[5]

There is one unifying theme of this subordinate/feminine language—it identifies the speaker as one who avoids exercising power. Reinforcing this perception of powerlessness, the non-assertive speaker:

- Is indirect and imprecise

- Uses more nonverbal communication (gesture and intonation)

- Rarely commits to an opinion

- Asks questions rather than makes assertions

- Tends to make emotional rather than logical statements

- Frequently asks for permission or approval

Because a subordinate, non-assertive style has been firmly established as appropriate "feminine" speech, a woman's speech patterns put her in a bind. When she speaks assertively or aggressively in a take-charge manner, she is considered unfeminine and pushy, but when she speaks in a traditional "feminine" (subordinate) way, she is not taken seriously and does not command authority. Damned if she does, and damned if she doesn't!

Civilized Assertiveness was designed to counteract this double bind. The communication research shows that when women are direct and assertive and also use traditional feminine speech habits that demonstrate concern for others, they are less likely to engender a backlash.[6] **In addition, women are equally influenced by both men and women they perceive as competent, but men are not. They are more influenced by competent men. However, men are also influenced by women they see as *both* competent and warm.**[7] These valuable findings point a way out of our dilemma. Along with developing assertiveness, we must be sure to hang on to our most positive, warm, and civilized traditional speech habits. We don't want to throw out the baby with the bath water!

If men and women are going to operate as equals for the first time in history, they will have to find new and better ways to talk to each other. They will need a common language that is both respectful and self-respecting. Fortunately, the building blocks for a more equitable language are already in place. I've studied hundreds of examples of traditional "male" and "female" speech, and an intriguing pattern emerges. The traditionally male speech habits which are *aggressive* parallel and **reinforce** the traditionally *passive* female speech habits. I came to think of this set of examples as competitive communication. It exploits differences by dividing people into polar categories: dominant/subordinate, master/slave, steamroller/wimp.

But there are traditional male speech habits which are *assertive*, not *aggressive*, and traditional female habits which are *civilized*, not *passive*. I came to think of this set as cooperative communication. It forms an ethical common language that connects rather than divides. It enables people to address differences constructively. It integrates the best of traditional male and female communication, the assertive and the civilized aspects, and discards the passive and aggressive aspects. Hence the term Civilized Assertiveness.

The Communication Quadrants

SUBORDINATE Traditional "Women" Talk			DOMINANT Traditional "Men" Talk
indirect tentative ingratiating apologetic overly polite self-diminishing no opinions nicey-nice overly responsive	PASSIVE	AGGRESSIVE	controlling judgmental combative critical interrupts puts down others boasts uses anger to get way bullies
sensitive inclusive non-judgmental considerate listens to others compliments speaks without hostility encourages collaborative	CIVILIZED	ASSERTIVE	direct speaks up stands up for ideas takes credit for work asks for feedback questions authority challenges misinformation action-oriented operates from choice

On the next page the quadrants are translated into the language of Civilized Assertiveness. Notice that the behaviors and traits from the top half of the Communication Quadrants need to be discarded. Those behaviors are passive and aggressive. The behaviors and traits from the bottom half of the grid are civilized and assertive—the behaviors we want to keep.[8]

DELETE
these behaviors

PASSIVE	AGGRESSIVE
tentative	controlling
indirect	judgmental
ingratiating	combative
apologetic	critical
overly polite	interrupts
self-diminishing	puts down others
no opinions	boasts
nicey-nice	uses anger to get way
overly responsive	bullies others

SAVE
these behaviors

CIVILIZED	ASSERTIVE
sensitive	direct
inclusive	speaks up
non-judgmental	stands up for ideas
considerate	takes credit for work
listens to others	asks for feedback
compliments	questions authority
speaks without hostility	challenges misinformation
encourages others	action-oriented
collaborative	operates from choice

ADD

Be continually on the lookout for positive skills and speech patterns to add to your repertoire. When you find assertive and civilized role models, closely observe them and appropriate the aspects of their expertise that are comfortable for you and make them your own.

The goal (for both men and women) is to use language only from the bottom half of the quadrants. It becomes the language of civilized assertiveness, combining the best and most effective from both "male" and "female" traditional speech. That is the way, in the words of an old song, to "accentuate the positive, eliminate the negative."

A recent, popular theory of gender communication tells us that male and female communication styles are so different that we might as well be from different planets. The theory holds that since there are pervasive gender differences in speech patterns, each sex must be rigorously coached in how to use the other's "gender dialect." If Dick and Jane can't shift into each other's mode of speaking, they are doomed to constantly misunderstand and misinterpret one another. An especially misleading part of this theory is the assumption that differences in communication patterns arise as an inevitable consequence of male/female traits.

Not so!

Men and women walk differently because their anatomy is different, and men and women use language differently because their culture is different. But anatomical differences are fixed and immutable; cultural differences are not. Our cultural patterns and language are learned behaviors that can be—*and constantly are*—modified, discarded, adapted, or replaced as the times, mores, and situations change. In this time of unprecedented social change for men and women, we need to heed the words attributed to popular American philosopher, George Carlin: "Men are from Earth; women are from Earth. Deal with it."

In this chapter, I have discussed "gender segregation" and its influence on our early socialization as boys and girls. In the next chapters, I will discuss further the differences between men's and women's language and teach you the language of civilized assertiveness that combines the best and most effective from both traditions. After we know from where we started, we can better know where (and how) to go.

Civilized Assertiveness reminds women of our rights and gives us the words, principles, and skills to reclaim what is ours. That is, our dignity, our self-respect, our time, and in some cases our health and sanity. What woman among us has not at one time or another put others' needs ahead of her own to the point of becoming burned out, resentful, or sick? Who has not, at some time, reflexively allowed others' views of us to color our self-image and lower our self-esteem? Civilized Assertiveness provides a template for standing up for ourselves and setting our boundaries. It allows us to establish our own personal power by giving us a clear, firm, and diplomatic way of talking to and interacting with others.

It has been understood for millennia that men and women have "gifts differing." We cannot be meaningfully compared to one another—we are simply different. As we go about examining our differences and how they intersect to affect our lives, we need to keep in mind one vital point: Our human differences are far outweighed by our human similarities. And because of this, we can be together, work together, and complement each other. It's time to accentuate our similarities, give up on fruitless comparisons of our differences, and figure out how best to make them work for us. Let's begin.

The Silent Woman

While touring England with my husband a few years ago, I noticed a charming inn called "The Silent Woman" and suggested we stop there for lunch. The minute he saw the sign, he got that infuriating look on his face which signals unflattering stereotypic thoughts about women. Being a very bright fellow, he decided many years ago to keep them to himself—however, "the look" gives him away. I've struggled for years to rise above it, but at some visceral level, I become irritated. I would like to get over my reaction for a couple of reasons. First, it's a deeply ingrained habit for him and it's not going to change (truth be known, I have my own unflattering thoughts), so it's a total waste of energy for me. But principally I want to ignore "the look" because he enjoys my reaction way too much.

In the case of "The Silent Woman," I reacted because I am acutely aware that the age-old prohibition against women speaking freely is still perpetuated and I know how subordinating it is for us. That women should remain silent in the presence of men—or at the very least, quiet and unassertive—is a sacred tradition. This is still honored in fundamentalist religions both here and abroad. The Bible instructs: [9]

- "I permit no woman to teach or to have authority over a man; she is to keep silent."

■ "Let the woman learn in silence with full
  submissiveness."

After World War II, most women left the "victory"
jobs they held in nearly every sector of the economy so
that the returning GIs could fill the vacancies. Women
were encouraged to return to the home, or if not already
married, to get a man and establish a home. There was a
plethora of articles and books advising them how to do it.
One such book by Charles D. Contreras, Ph.D., *How to
Fascinate Men,* counseled, without a trace of irony,

> ... The fact must always be kept in mind
> that nothing a woman may do to attract
> attention will be of much avail, if there is in
> her manner, voice or apparel, the suggestion of
> strength, manliness, efficiency, ability, or
> severity. The woman who is obviously able to
> look after her own interest, without male help,
> cannot attract favorable attention from men,
> no matter what arts and devices she employs.[10]

As women enter this shiny new century, this brightly
burning torch has been handed to traditionalist guru John
Gray of *Men are From Mars, Women are from Venus* fame.
With over 70 books and products on the market, he is available for inspiration and guidance on a wide variety of sub-
jects, but two glistening threads run through most of them:

■ A woman is a vulnerable little thing and a man
  needs to take care of his little lady: "Deep down
  inside her is a scared little girl who is afraid of
  opening up and being hurt and needs your
  kindness and compassion."

■ A woman needs to hold her tongue: "On Venus it is considered a loving gesture to offer advice. But on Mars it is not. Any attempt to change him is counter productive. The secret of empowering a man is never to try to change or improve him." [11]

Dear Gentlemen,

We wanted to send our thanks for your concern and advice. We know that the behavior of many men has been, at least in part, motivated by a perceived need to take care of women. We realize in your eyes, a woman needs a wise and caring father, husband, minister, boss, governor, senator, president, who can make the important decisions and policies, and shield her from the more unpleasant realities of life. Again, for any of your past genuine concerns, we thank you.

But for now and in the future—no thanks.

In this new century, we will be needing something quite different from you. In order to understand this, I want to tell you what women are currently doing, as I think you have somehow missed it. Today, women have an increasingly large stake in our society and in the world. In 2000, of employees ages 25 to 34, women were:[12]

■ 46% of the workforce
■ 65% of the service occupation positions
■ 50% of professional and technical occupations
■ 51% of executive, administrative, and managerial positions
■ 30% of lawyers
■ 10% of engineers
■ 15% of the armed forces

In the 21st Century what we need from you is support and respect—just as we have supported and respected you for so long. We need to be partners, not subordinates; co-pilots, not crew; people, not just women. We need and intend to be "not just our little feminine selves, but our whole big fully human selves." And as your partners, we need to work, love, laugh, play, and look at the stars.

Respectfully,

Judith Doe, et al.

Your Communication Rights

*A*s Nora said in Ibsen's *A Doll's House,* "Above every-thing else I am a human being." Equality boils down to women defining themselves not in female terms, but in human terms. When women were defined mainly by their duty to others, they had little need to ponder the scope of their rights. Today, as we pursue our own interests and develop new competencies, we urgently need to exercise our fundamental human rights.

In the rush of daily life, many of us haven't taken the time to think about what our rights are and how we express them. The following assessment gives you this opportunity. By responding to these everyday situations, you will assess how you react when your rights have been violated and how well you respect the rights of others. Becoming fully conscious of your basic human rights paves the way for equal participation in the world.

TAKING STOCK OF YOUR RIGHTS

Read each statement and respond as honestly as you can. Your answers should reflect your current attitudes and behavior, not what you did in the past or hope to do in the future. Circle the number that most accurately describes you. Rate each question from one to five:

1 = Almost never
2 = Somewhat or sometimes
3 = Half the time
4 = Usually or a good deal
5 = Almost always

1. I'm comfortable stating my
   opinion in a discussion.   1   2   3   4   5

2. I am critical and judgmental of others.   1   2   3   4   5

3. When someone talks during a
   movie, I ask her to stop.   1   2   3   4   5

4. I lose my temper quickly.   1   2   3   4   5

5. I insist that my partner shares
   the housework.   1   2   3   4   5

6. I keep arguing even when
   the other person wants to quit.   1   2   3   4   5

7. I speak up when I'm treated
   disrespectfully or unjustly.   1   2   3   4   5

8. When I'm mad, I swear, yell,
   or belittle.   1   2   3   4   5

9. When I disagree with someone,
   I am able to say so.   1   2   3   4   5

10. I jump in and tell others what to
do or make decisions for them.   1   2   3   4   5

11. I can say no to excessive
requests from family or friends.   1   2   3   4   5

12. I intimidate others to get them to
do what I want.   1   2   3   4   5

13. I maintain eye contact when
listening or speaking to others.   1   2   3   4   5

14. I believe my answers and solutions
are the best.   1   2   3   4   5

15. When a borrowed item is not
returned, I ask for it.   1   2   3   4   5

16. When speaking with others, I try
to control the conversation.   1   2   3   4   5

17. I'm not afraid to express what I feel. 1   2   3   4   5

18. I find it hard to commend or
compliment others.   1   2   3   4   5

19. I am able to say no to unreasonable
requests from my boss.   1   2   3   4   5

20. I finish other people's sentences. 1   2   3   4   5

Look back over the questionnaire and note the pattern of odd and even numbered questions. Circle the odd numbered questions: They assess passive and assertive responses. For these questions, 1, 3, 5, 7, 9, etc., a low score indicates a passive response, and a higher number indicates an assertive response. For example, in statement number 1, "I speak up when I'm treated disrespectfully or unjustly," a 1 or 2 would be a passive

response, while a 4 or 5 would be an assertive response. For the even numbered questions, 2, 4, 6, 8, etc., a high number indicates an aggressive response, and a lower number indicates a civilized response. In statement number 2, "I am critical and judgmental of others," a 4 or 5 would be an aggressive response, while a 1 or 2 is not passive but rather a civilized way of behaving that respects other people's rights. This mindful and respectful approach to life is the other side of assertiveness. Hence the concept of Civilized Assertiveness.

The assessment identifies a number of behaviors and situations that occur in our everyday lives. When you look at the pattern of your responses, you'll clearly see that being assertive isn't an either/or characteristic, but that assertiveness is "situationally specific." You can be assertive in one situation and not in another; on one occasion but not another; and with one person but not another. The trick is to build on your areas of strength and develop new communication habits that make you more assertive in all phases of your life.

You will probably identify some behaviors that you particularly want to change. Pick out three and list them on the following page. Choose one or several to focus on. Phrase the statement in positive and active terms in the present tense. For example:

"I refuse requests from my boss when they are unreasonable."

"I am able to compliment and praise others."

"I allow others to make their own decisions."

THREE ASSERTIVE GOALS

1. _____

2. _____

3. _____

Realize that you won't learn new assertive habits instantly or perfectly. Give yourself permission to be awkward and self-conscious, to come on too strong and occasionally to lapse. The commitment is to keep on working at the change in behavior until it finally becomes a habit. (See Five Steps to Assertive Habits on page 96.)

YOUR PERSONAL BILL OF RIGHTS

The situations in "Taking Stock of Your Rights" are everyday examples that call for exercising your rights and respecting the rights of others. Basic rights are simply universal human standards for how to treat each other ethically. They are fundamental to a democratic way of life. These rights flow from a framework that is as old as human striving for equality and were articulated over 200 years ago in the American Declaration of Independence. Exercising communication rights is a declaration of independence at a personal level.

The universality of fundamental rights was made even more explicit and personal in 1945 when the United Nations proclaimed a common standard for all people of all nations in the Universal Declaration of Human Rights. It recognized that "the inherent dignity and equal and inalienable rights of all

members of the human family is the foundation of freedom, justice and peace in the world," and proclaimed the universal right to "freedom of thought, conscience, opinion and expression."

Considered in this light, exercising human rights is as much a duty as a right. This duty is to the larger human community. Our assertiveness actively affirms basic standards of behavior necessary for civilized relationships. The equality that we are establishing is not an equality of status, aptitude, or ability, but an equality of fundamental rights as human beings. It is the one universal and abiding bulwark against bigotry, intolerance, and discrimination of all kinds.

The ten personal rights on the following page are based on recent research in assertiveness and are rooted in universal democratic rights.[13]

Personal Bill of Rights

1. **To express thoughts and feelings** *without qualification or apology.*

2. **To have thoughts, feelings and rights respected.**

3. **To be listened to and taken seriously** *by peer, subordinate, boss, friend or foe.*

4. **To ask for what one wants** *whether or not others think the request is sensible, logical, or prudent.*

5. **To make mistakes** *as long as you take responsibility for them.*

6. **To ask for information** *no matter how basic or self-evident.*

7. **To say NO** *without apology or excuse.*

8. **To make a decision on one's own terms** *without feeling compelled to justify it or state the reasons for making it.*

9. **To not feel guilty** *about choosing your needs over someone else's.*

10. **To choose not to be assertive.**

NOTES

Communication Styles:
Doormat, Steamroller, or Pillar?

> We cannot put off living until we are
>
> ready—life is fired at us point-blank.
>
> – Jose Ortega y Gasset

s life hurls toward us, we have three basic ways to respond:

1. Stand back or give way (passive)
2. Push forward reflexively or offensively (aggressive)
3. Stand firm or step forward in a mindful way (assertive)

A quick look at the literal definitions of each term points up some important distinctions and highlights the confusion surrounding the concept of assertiveness.

Dictionary Definitions

Aggressive adj.
1. Inclined to move or act in a hostile fashion.
2. Assertive; bold; enterprising.

Aggress v.i.
To start an attack or quarrel.

Passive adj.
1. Receiving or subjected to an action without responding or initiating an action in return.
2. Not participating or acting; submissive; inert.

Pass v.t.
To relinquish a right.

Assertive adj.
Inclined to bold assertion; positive.

Assert v.t.
1. To state or express positively; affirm.
2. To defend or maintain (one's rights, for example). To express oneself forcefully or boldly.

Considering the two dictionary definitions for the adjective "aggressive," it's easy to see why the terms "aggressive" and "assertive" are often confused in everyday conversation.

To add to the confusion, when most of us think of the concept of assertiveness often we mistakenly visualize a continuum. In our mind's eye we tend to see passivity at one end, aggression at the other, and assertiveness closer to, and a milder form of, aggression.

But there is no continuum. Instead there are two distinctly separate categories. The passive and aggressive characteristics reinforce each other and are compatible in a dysfunctional way, making the passive-aggressive interactions hard to change. The assertive characteristics, however, form a healthy and functional realm of their own.

PASSIVE

- Goes off in a huff to manipulate
- Sighs a lot
- Says he or she is angry while smiling
- Tries to sit on both sides of the fence to avoid conflict
- Is afraid to take risks
- Shows stage fright when speaking in front of a group
- Clams up when he or she feels treated unfairly
- Asks permission when it isn't necessary
- Complains instead of taking action
- Buys approval by appearing selfless, a good sport

AGGRESSIVE

- Puts others down
- May respond too vigorously, making a negative impression
- Expresses ideas and opinions strongly
- Is often first and very competitive
- Doesn't ever think he or she is wrong
- Takes over a group
- Exhibits bossy, pushy behavior
- Takes charge, task-oriented, gets important things done
- Moves into people's space, overpowers
- Jumps on others, pushes people around

ASSERTIVE

- Operates from choice
- Knows what is needed and develops a plan to get it
- Is action-oriented
- Demonstrates firmness
- Is initially trusting
- Assumes responsibility for self
- Has realistic expectations
- Emphasizes the positive nature of self and of others
- Deals with others fairly and justly
- Behaves with consistency
- Takes proactive positions
- Takes appropriate action toward filling needs and wants without denying rights of others

Looking at the lists on the previous page,[14] you can see how the passive and aggressive approaches tend to reinforce each other. When there is a shift in power, the roles are easily reversed. Sometimes the two sets of characteristics combine to form a third approach called passive-aggressive.

For example, Susan, an office manager in a small company, feels overworked, underpaid, and put down by a boss she describes as a steamroller. She complains to friends and co-workers that she is unappreciated and treated badly. But at review time, although seething inside, she smiles brightly and accepts small salary increases without comment.

Susan's style is to ignore insulting behavior and she rarely says "no", no matter how unreasonable the request. She does, however, "forget" to follow up on key requests, calls in sick on days when her absence would be particularly disruptive, and frequently makes sarcastic comments about her boss and the low wage she is paid. Her behavior is passive because she does not ask for a change, and at the same time it is aggressive because she uses sabotage and sarcasm.

Review the lists and you'll find it is clear that an interaction between two people using predominantly aggressive approaches or two people using predominantly passive approaches would be tough going. Two aggressives would be in constant competition and conflict. Two passives would have trouble getting anything going to begin with. ("After you, Alfonso.") This may explain why passives and aggressives have such an affinity for each other. The ongoing interaction between a predominantly aggressive person and a predominantly passive person creates an authoritarian relationship.

Authoritarian and competitive relationships focus on issues of power and control. Winston Churchill succinctly defined the authoritarian personality as being "either at your feet or at your throat." The central questions are:

- Who's in charge?
- How can I demonstrate superiority?
- Who's stronger?
- Who has power over whom?
- What's my status?

In this model, relationships are viewed primarily as power struggles which have only winners and losers. People and events are divided into polar categories: dominant/subordinate, master/slave, boss/underling, them/us.

In a cooperative and assertive relationship, the questions are open-ended and focus on differences in positive and constructive ways:

- What special strengths do each of us bring to the interaction?
- What are each of our needs, interests, and skills?
- How do we both get our needs met?
- How do we generate possibilities and options that allow for this?
- How do we compromise and negotiate?
- When resources are limited, and when push comes to shove, how do we allocate wisely and make hard choices based on fair and decent standards?

The table on the following page[15] vividly summarizes the main factors for each of the passive, aggressive, and assertive styles, as well as the passive-aggressive (also known as manipulative) style.

FACTOR	STYLES			
	PASSIVE	AGGRESSIVE	PASSIVE-AGGRESSIVE	ASSERTIVE
TREATMENT of RIGHTS	Gives up own	Usurps others	Sneakily usurps others	Maintains own
METAPHOR	Doormat	Steamroller	Doormat with spikes	Pillar
VERBAL BEHAVIOR	Qualifies, apologizes	Blames, accuses	Uses sarcasm indirectly	Speaks mind openly
NONVERBAL BEHAVIOR	Averted gaze, soft voice, cowers	Stares, loud voice, invades others' space	Sideways glance, sarcastic tone, shifts limbs	Direct gaze, varied voice, balanced
RESPONSE	Flight	Fight	Hit and Run	Engagement

The approach we choose in dealing with each other reflects the choices we make about whose needs we honor and whose rights we respect.

RESPECT FOR RIGHTS			
	PASSIVE	AGGRESSIVE	MANIPULATIVE	ASSERTIVE
OWN RIGHTS	–	+	–	+
OTHER'S RIGHTS	+	–	–	+

Only the assertive approach respects both our own rights and those of others. Only the assertive approach honors our own needs as well as the needs of others. Only the assertive approach mindfully assesses the situation and strives to negotiate a satisfactory outcome for all.

NOTES

Personal Checks and Balance

The indispensable element for establishing balanced relationships is a clear understanding of what you want and need. For many women this is not a simple task. Women have been socialized to be the responders, the nurturers, the caretakers. Some aspects of this behavior—listening, recognizing needs, and empathizing—are valuable skills that are important to retain. But some other aspects of this nurturing behavior need to be modified or discarded.

Traditionally, women have been so busy automatically responding to the needs and requests of others that they rarely get around to thinking about what they need or want in a situation or in a relationship. Too often they automatically make commitments without really questioning what they're getting into—and then live to regret it! In order to function effectively, they need to modify this tendency. The personal checks described in this chapter were developed to help curb the strong inclination to say yes before thinking through the consequences.

The personal checks of Civilized Assertiveness keep you from mindlessly allowing yourself to be used or manipulated by others. Equally important, they protect you from your own desire to be "nice," a socialization which leads you to do things

you neither want nor need to do. The personal checks force you to be conscious of the cost of compliance. They help you set limits and say no.

The personal checks show you how to balance—not subjugate—your wants, needs, and goals with the wants, needs, and requests of others. Being assertive doesn't mean being overbearing or saying "No" to everything; neither does it mean saying "Yes" to everything.

THE PERSONAL CHECKS

There are two personal checks: The internal check focuses on your feelings, and the external check focuses on facts. Rather than responding to a request immediately, first perform the personal checks. They force you to pause and think about what the request means to you and what it entails. It is essential that you pause briefly before saying anything in any interaction with another person. This gives you time to ask yourself one simple but powerful question.

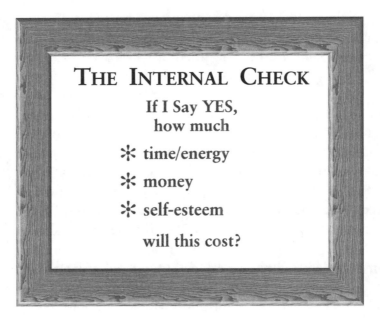

THE INTERNAL CHECK

If I Say YES,
how much

✳ time/energy

✳ money

✳ self-esteem

will this cost?

This question allows you to handle interactions with your family, friends, lovers, fellow employees, subordinates, and bosses in a balanced way. You can make real decisions only when the stakes of your commitment are clear. When you complete your check, you're in a position to decide if you want to comply and if so, to what extent. At this point you can make an educated choice. Make the internal check your first step in order to guide your remaining choices and actions.

The external check is a straightforward process of making sure you have all the pertinent facts before you obligate yourself to any new task or responsibility. This skill is essential for effective and balanced interactions at work, but is equally useful in personal situations when someone makes a request.

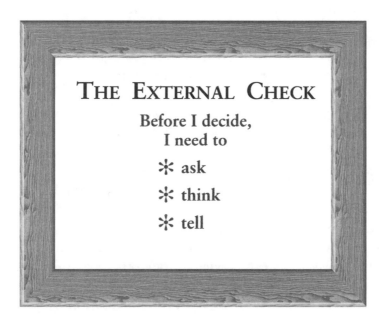

THE EXTERNAL CHECK
Before I decide,
I need to
* ask
* think
* tell

The external check keeps you from prematurely agreeing to tasks or projects which you haven't had time to think through.

There are three basic steps that take you through the process.

1. **ASK** specifically what would be expected of you. You need to be clear about three things before committing:

   ✳ What is the SCOPE?

   ✳ What RESOURCES are available?

   ✳ When is the DEADLINE?

2. When you are clear about the scope, resources, and deadline, **THINK** through what a commitment to the request would mean for you. Do this through an internal check: If I say yes, how much time, energy, and self-esteem will it cost?

3. **TELL** what your position is regarding the request in terms of your current commitments.

For example, a colleague or boss says, "I'm counting on your help in getting this proposal out by next week." Instead of automatically responding "Oh, sure" or "I don't know… I'm really swamped," you would say, "I'm not clear what you need from me. When can we sit down and go over what this would involve?"

When you meet, get the specifics on the scope of the project, the resources available, and the deadline. Think through the personal costs and the impact on other work commitments. Be sure to clearly define for yourself your other commitments so that you can factor them into your time and energy priorities.

As you begin to learn the skills of Civilized Assertiveness, you will need to slow down most conversations (at work and at home) so that you are truly aware of what's going on. You need to understand the sequence of events and ask questions so that you have adequate information to make decisions in your best interest. This process also has the by-product of conveying competence.

GARY LA CROIX

A HABIT OF SUSPENDED RESPONSE

Many of us have learned our lessons in civility too well. We say we don't mind when we do mind. We say "It's no trouble," when indeed it's a great deal of trouble.

It's not "civility" when you automatically give in or go along to get along. It's called speaking before thinking, at best, or being a real wimp, at worst. Automatic civility can be as damaging to a relationship as automatic aggression. When you reflexively volunteer for things that you later regret, one of two things happens: You carry through on the commitment, but are resentful, or you don't carry through and the other person is resentful. Either way it's a no-win situation.

The remedy is to check your natural and quite commendable urge to agree immediately to help someone out. Instead of responding immediately and automatically, consciously pause and conduct an internal check before you say anything at all. You may decide to go ahead with your initial agreeable response, but this time you will have mindfully chosen to make it.

Here's how it works:

A friend or spouse says: "You wouldn't mind dropping this off for me, would you? It's right on your way."

STEP 1: Internal Check Pause

Ask yourself, "What's this going to cost me in terms of time, money, or self-esteem?"

STEP 2: Then, you answer simply,

"That would not be convenient for me" or

"I'm really rushed. I just won't have the time."

Do not add, "sorry" or "I'd like to, but..." Apologies are unnecessary.

Suspending your response is particularly important when coping with aggressive and manipulative people. Their success depends on their victim's automatic civility and good manners. The more courteous and polite you are, the more vulnerable you are to their wiles. The more you explain or apologize, the more open you are to manipulation. When you have reason to suspect that you are dealing with such a person, your most effective safeguard is simply to remain in a state of suspended civility. Remember that just because you may ask some questions in an external check doesn't mean you have to say yes to a request any more than you would have to buy a car after asking the salesperson for details about it.

SUSPENDED CIVILITY

Don't say anything...

Just pause and

think!

A Special Word About the Phrase: "I'm Sorry"

When I teach three-part workshops, I assign field-work to be done during the week between the first and second class: Listen for the phrase, "I'm sorry"—

■ Observe how and when men say "I'm sorry."

■ Don't say it this week.

The discussion that results the second evening is most enlightening. As far as observing the men goes, the answers range from "Not as often as I do, but some,"(rare) to "I didn't hear the guys at work use it all, but my husband said it a few of times" (frequent). The reports from the women about their own use range from, "no problem for me—I don't say it much anyway" (rare), to "I was amazed how often I said it, but I did catch myself and by the end of the week was able to get through a whole day without saying it" (frequent). My favorite example from my classes came from ever-sorry Samantha: "I was at the supermarket and I dropped a zucchini on the floor and automatically said, 'Oh, I'm so sorry'." Things have come to a sorry pass when you are apologizing to your vegetables!

When Monty Python alumnus Eric Idle was asked in a *Vanity Fair* interview what phrase he overused most,

he said, "'I'm sorry.' It's an overused and meaningless phrase." We use it for everything from comforting a widow to bumping into someone in a store to asking someone to repeat a something we didn't quite catch. Are we actually apologetic for that stuff? If we are, there are better ways to apologize, and there are indeed better ways to excuse oneself or ask for clarification:

Pardon me.

Come again?

OOPS! My mistake.

Please forgive me...

I apologize for...

"I'm sorry" should be used only at funerals. The S-word is pretty limp in any other situation. It implies that you could have helped or done something about whatever happened but you didn't, or that you're not about to help resolve an issue. Worst of all, many of us—such as Samantha, the zucchini apologizer—use the phrase mindlessly and frequently (the prize-winner in my classes was 47 times a week!) This overuse marks us as passive and subordinate. The statement "I'm sorry" only expresses a state, but "I apologize" has an action verb in it, indicating you are doing or can do something about it.

So from now on, no more "I'm sorry."

Try it for a day, then a week.

Then try it for life.

NOTES

Principles and Skills

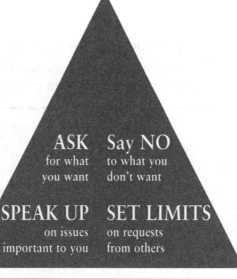

ASK
for what
you want

Say NO
to what you
don't want

SPEAK UP
on issues
important to you

SET LIMITS
on requests
from others

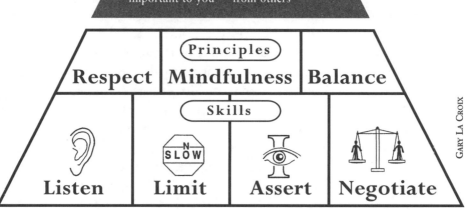

| Respect | Principles | Balance |
| | Mindfulness | |

Skills

| Listen | Limit | Assert | Negotiate |

GARY LA CROIX

*I*n a nutshell, Civilized Assertiveness requires taking only three steps:

---

1 First, ask for what you want and refuse what you don't want, in an honest, straightforward and considerate manner.

2 Second, stand up for your convictions and hold your own in conflict situations without becoming aggressive, manipulative, or unpleasant.

3 Third, set limits with aggressive or needy people and turn down excessive, inconvenient, or inappropriate requests from others.

Easy to state, but how do you apply these three steps of Civilized Assertiveness in real world situations? How do you find the words to be assertive? How do you remain civilized when others are making outrageous demands of you and/or acting outrageously? How do you respond assertively and civilly without sounding martyred, angry, or ugly? And finally, the million dollar question, how do you say "no" comfortably?

Most of us think of civility as politeness and good manners, behaviors designed to please, or at least not to give offense. Those are the surface behaviors of civility and they're important. But there is also a deep structure to civility. It is those habits of heart and mind that allow us to be cooperative rather than self-centered—to be able, when necessary, to put what is right for the common good ahead of our own self interest. It is these attitudes and inclinations that raise society above barbarism and allow us to live together peacefully. Citizen, civil, civility—all three of these

terms are interconnected. Unfortunately, the concept of civility has gotten muddy through the years and sometimes we mistake civility for passivity and doing what is polite with doing what is right. We really need to sort through our training and inclinations and tease out the difference between what is passive and what is truly civilized behavior.

Civility is ethical behavior which encourages us to relate to each other humanely. It is the opposite of aggression. Assertiveness encompasses behaviors that allow us to pursue our interests and stand up for our rights without infringing on the rights of others or encouraging others to stomp on ours. It is the opposite of passivity. Passivity shows that we do not respect ourselves. Aggression shows that we do not respect others' rights. Either way we diminish ourselves. That's why it's so important that civility and assertiveness go hand-in-hand.

There are three guiding principles that flow from this deep core of civility—respect, mindfulness, and balance. When we have acted according to these three principles, we can be sure that our behavior has been civilized and assertive.

Following are the three principles with a set of questions to test your behavior in each area. Again, as with the Taking Stock of Your Rights assessment on page 32, answer these questions as you are today, not as you hope to be.

THE GUIDING PRINCIPLES OF CIVILIZED ASSERTIVENESS

RESPECT

The word respect can refer to an admiring attitude or courteous treatment of another person or group. Civilized Assertiveness uses it in the second sense: to avoid violation of and show consideration for others. An ethical approach to relationships demands that we be respectful of all others at all times, even when they are opposing us. This is sometimes extremely hard to do and occasionally even the most disciplined of us fail.

✻   Do you believe that respect is a fundamental human right due every human being? Or do you give respect conditionally depending on a person's authority, status, affiliation, or agreement with your beliefs?

✻   Even when you dislike, disagree with, or disapprove of the other person, do you speak to him respectfully? Or do you feel justified in speaking abruptly, rudely, sarcastically, or condescendingly?

✻   When involved in a conflict, can you listen to the other person's point of view in a non-judgmental way? Or do you attack with blaming, shaming, or discounting?

✻   Do you maintain your own self-respect by refusing to let others dominate, manipulate, or take advantage of you?

MINDFULNESS

Mindfulness means we continuously create new ways to categorize experiences, as opposed to a rigid reliance on set ways of thinking—a hardening of the categories.[16] A mindful state calls for openness to new information and other points of view. When we are receptive to new and different perspectives, we are able to generate more options for understanding situations, solving problems, and developing creative solutions.

✻   Do you often find yourself saying "I can't believe I did that," or "I didn't mean to say that," or "I don't know what came over me?" (Sure signs that you have been mindless.)

✻   Are you generally aware and tuned in to what's going on around you in the present moment? Or are you often distracted and on automatic pilot?

✳   When others ask questions or make requests, do you pause and think things through before responding? Or do you react instantly?

✳   Do you actively try to imagine how issues and situations look to other people? Or do you tend to see things only from your own perspective? Do you sit there thinking how dumb or wrong they are?

BALANCE

✳   Do you weigh the opinions, rights, and interests of others against your own? Or do you single-mindedly push for your opinion, your way, or your advantage? (Conversely, do you diminish yourself by automatically giving in to others?)

✳   Do you balance your right to say no and set limits with generous efforts to meet the other person's needs?

✳   Do you balance telling others what you don't like with telling them what you do like? (At work, what you depend upon and like; in personal relationships, what you depend upon and cherish.)

✳   Do you strive to establish egalitarian relationships that at times may favor one person over the other, but in the long run are equal and fair?

Respect, mindfulness, and balance are the three standards of civility that guarantee we are speaking and acting with integrity. Often it's their absence that underscores their importance. When we look back on situations that we've not handled well, we usually realize we have violated one or more of

these principles. Just as the three principles keep you grounded in civility, there are four powerful communication skills that keep you grounded in assertiveness: Listen, Limit, Assert, Negotiate.

Listen is the first skill and the foundation of the other three. In order to communicate effectively, we must have a clear understanding of the situation. Often we get involved in something before we've taken the trouble to listen attentively and understand what the other person is really saying. Without a true picture of how the other person sees a situation, we often defend ourselves when we don't need to, discuss the wrong issues, or solve the wrong problems.

The second skill is **Limit.** Most relationships involve conflicting wants, needs, and rights; the goal is to be fair and balanced in working them out. But we cannot honor the principle of balance unless we are able to refuse requests and stick to our own agendas. Healthy adults do not feel guilty about saying no, but many women do! Without the ability to say no and set limits, we cannot fully live our lives. It's high time to get rid of the guilt and truly be ourselves.

Assert is the third skill. It has three parts:

1) Asking directly for what you want by telling people what, when, and why you need something;

2) Stating how other people's behavior affects you and how you honestly feel about it; and

3) Asking for feedback, clarification, or cooperation when you need it. Silence is leaden, not golden, when it comes to Civilized Assertiveness.

The final skill, **Negotiate,** integrates and builds on the other three skills. It allows us to work out effective and ethical solutions to the dilemmas that are an inevitable part of everyday life. In large measure, our success in life depends upon our success as a negotiator.

These four crucial communication skills are presented in Chapters 8 through 11. They sound simple enough. But as you will discover in the following chapters, these skills do not come naturally. They require new strategies, practical techniques, specific language, and practice, practice, practice! Mastering these skills will enable you to stand up for yourself without sounding defensive, ask for what you need without being pushy or apologetic, and get more of what you want without exploiting others.

NOTES

EIGHT

Listen

istening is what most of us pretend to do while we are waiting for our turn to talk. It is a rather disorderly process. Our attention weaves in and out, our mind wanders to its own preoccupation, and we often fake attention. The way in which the human mind processes information allows—in fact actually encourages—this. People speak at roughly 125-200 words a minute, but their minds are able to process information a great deal more quickly—roughly 500 words a minute. The added *free* time the mind has is usually frittered away on unrelated distractions.

Active listening is the important first step in Civilized Assertiveness. When we learn to listen *actively*, we learn to use this *free* time to focus total attention on the speaker's message. The purpose is to ensure that we understand what the other person is saying so we have a clear picture of the situation. Without this, we risk defending the wrong points, dealing with the wrong issues, or wasting time on unnecessary details.

Active listening is a very different process than the way we usually listen. There are two basic activities that keep us focused:

✳   Summarize or paraphrase your understanding of the other's viewpoint.

✳ Ask questions for clarification, more information, or to get specific examples.

Active listening through asking questions and paraphrasing is powerful for three reasons.

1. It is the quickest and most effective way to let the speaker know that you have understood a viewpoint. For instance, when a speaker goes over the same point again and again, it's often because it's very important to that particular person and they think (perhaps mistakenly) that you haven't gotten it. Summarizing what has been said shows that you understand.

2. It immediately gets the speaker involved and responsible for her part of the discussion. If you haven't understood the speaker's position correctly, she can tell you so and restate it. In addition, active listening may cause speakers to face the fact that they are not being clear or have contradicted themselves.

    Example:

    Listener: Jim, are you saying that Sara really isn't competent to handle the new account?

    Speaker: No, it's not that she's not competent to do it, it's just that she is overloaded already and we shouldn't pile on anything more.

3. It demonstrates that you respect another's right to state opinions. It shows you are trying to see the world through her eyes. Later, when you want to have your say, you have already earned the right to have your point of view heard. The deceptively simple act of listening is one of the most powerful means of showing respect.

Example:

You: Sam, let me make sure I understand you. The way you see this is that we already have more work than we can do and we can't service any more clients, because we won't be able to maintain our quality control. Consequently, you think we ought to refuse the account. Is this pretty much what you're saying?

Sam: Yes it is.

You: Okay—I see this a little differently. I think we can handle it, and here's why…

It would be very difficult for Sam to respond negatively. He would have to be playing real hardball to say, "No, I'm not interested in hearing your point of view."

A sometimes difficult part of active listening involves temporarily giving up your position so that you can truly look through the other person's eyes and temporarily enter the speaker's reality. You must momentarily suspend your ego. It takes a very solid ego to be able to do this. It also puts your viewpoint to the test. We view the world through lenses that have been colored by our different experiences: childhood, families, education, experiences, and so on. Our different backgrounds, temperaments, and experiences often make us interpret the same situation in contrary ways.

For example, Ted and Sandra, a newly-married couple, are having problems handling their household finances. Ted, who grew up in a poor family, is a super penny-pincher to the point of being someone who is unpleasant to take on a shopping trip, even to a discount store. Sandra, who grew up in a wealthy family and

enjoyed many luxuries, is more extravagant. There are constant fights about family finances, which leave both of them tense and unhappy. For him, money is for saving and for her, money is for spending. Some months they fall short and run up credit card balances with high interest. Even when they get an occasional windfall they argue over "the right way" to use it.

To date, when they have tried to discuss their problem, Ted tends to moralize and challenge Sandra: "You need to be more respectful of money—a penny saved is a penny earned. When are you going to grow up and act like a financially responsible adult?" In turn, Sandra usually psychoanalyzes and criticizes Ted for being too serious: "What's the sense of having any money if you can't have a little fun? Just because you had a tough time when you were young doesn't mean we can't have any fun...or does it?!" These conversations end in more anger or hurt feelings and a renewed conviction that the other is wrong, impossible to talk to, and pig-headed.

These are the occasions when Ted and Sandra need to use active listening to the fullest. If she can get her ego out of the way and truly listen, Sandra probably can benefit from understanding Ted's need for security, his virtue of planning ahead, and his sound financial sense. If he can do the same, Ted probably can benefit from Sandra's ability to enjoy and stay in the moment. Through calmer discussions Ted may find that indeed he does want to loosen up and have some fun. Sandra may find that she can be happy and enjoy herself without living so extravagantly.

You don't have to know someone's full history to understand her present opinion or viewpoint. But you do have to know and acknowledge that people come from different places and that this often causes them to see situations quite differently than you do.

Another benefit of learning how to actively listen to another person is that it tangibly tests your convictions. If you have conscientiously measured your perception against his and

find your convictions still remain strong and true, then you have gained greater awareness. If your convictions don't hold up, then it's time to re-evaluate your position.

Active listening takes attention and energy, as well as confidence and courage. The most efficient communication strategy is to match the amount of attention and energy expended to the importance of the situation.

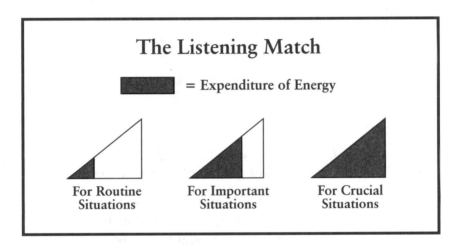

1. **Routine Listening, Level I,** is what most of us do without much focus or directed attention. It works for commonplace situations when we aren't getting new information or don't need to do much out of the ordinary. It doesn't tax us or challenge us and we go along pretty much on automatic pilot.

   Example: You're driving a car and your passenger says, "Turn left."

   When the stakes are higher and we need to be mindful of what's going on because there will be significant consequences, we need to move to Level II or Level III.

2. **Active Listening, Level II,** uses the *free* time to focus full attention on the speaker's message.

    ■ Paraphrase information to yourself
    ■ Make connections between what the speaker is saying and what you already know
    ■ Acknowledge the speaker's ideas by paraphrasing and/or summarizing the content
    ■ Interpret nonverbal clues
    ■ Ask clarifying questions and check perceptions

    Example: You are driving and your passenger says, "The bridge on Downing Street is out. You need to take another route."

    Active Listening

    To self: "Oh yes, that's right. Now how did I go the other day? Logan?"

    To passenger: "Thanks for reminding me. I think Logan would probably be best. Or do you have a better way?"

3. **Active Listening, Level III,** has the listener intensely focused on the speaker. Use the techniques from Level II above and in addition,

    ■ Encourage with eye contact, nods, and statements such as, "Yes, go on" or "Tell me more"
    ■ Estimate the speaker's underlying feelings and ask if you're right
    ■ Ask open-ended questions to encourage discussion

    Example: Your best friend says, "I'm scared of driving after my big accident."

Active Listening

To self: "I remember that; it really shook her up and she hasn't been quite herself since."

To friend: "I bet that has been really tough on you—so scary. It takes a long time to get over something like that. How are you doing now?"

Using these techniques and mastering the art of active listening takes practice and perseverance, but the pay-off is more accurate information, a clearer understanding of situations and events, and better relationships.

When you listen actively to another person, you demonstrate that the message has been received and understood. This gives the other person a sense of closure so that he or she can relax for a time and then turn full attention on you (as you become the speaker). The act of listening itself shows respect and when someone feels heard and understood, you can actually learn more from him and help work through the problem more effectively. He doesn't feel as if he has to keep making his point or trying to be heard. Instead, he can continue with his own train of thought.

Listening is the foundation skill and it is only the prelude to exercising your other skills and rights. Don't forget to go on with the next part—taking your turn to be heard. After you've carefully listened to someone, it is then time to use your other skills. Too many women listen to others and then forget to balance the equation.

Not only does active listening have a beneficial effect on the other person and on the conversation, it has a positive and calming effect on you, as well. Research measuring physiological responses to human dialogue has shown that when people are listening actively, their blood pressure falls and their body relaxes.[17] This is a remarkable perk—when we listen to others, we gain not only information, but some tranquility as well.

NOTES

NINE

Limit

The number one problem for women in my Civilized Assertiveness classes is saying no. Sad, because it is such a positive and freeing word. This chapter helps you slow down any urge to say yes and demonstrates six ways to say no.

When we are unsure about whether we can or want to do something, most of us tend to say yes. It is a great deal easier, more natural, and more appealing. Because most requests aren't stated very clearly, it is no wonder that the communication deck is strongly stacked against saying no.

Simply realizing that there are ramifications even to simple requests and that it's appropriate to be uncertain about how to respond are important first steps to becoming more assertive in dealing with others. As you become mindful of the dynamics of assertive communication, you become clear that you have every right—in fact an obligation—to take your time and to get more information. This is why the Personal Checks are so important and useful. They encourage us to develop a habit of suspended response.

**A HABIT OF
SUSPENDED RESPONSE**

When you are unclear whether you can or want to comply, don't say yes or no. Instead, SLOW DOWN AND THINK:

1. Ask for more information:
   - "Can you tell me more about it?"
   - "I don't think I'm following you. Would you go over that again?"
   - "Could you give me some more of the details/more of an overview?"
   - "Well, let's see: What else can you tell me about it?"
   - "Let me make sure I understand. This is…"
   - "Hmm. What's involved in this?"

2. Don't commit—buy some time:
   - "I'll want to think this through."
   - "I'll need some time to think about this."
   - "Let me think about this."
   - "Let me check my schedule and get back to you."

This response is most effective when followed by a specific time: "*…and I'll get back to you by this afternoon (or Friday or next week)."*

When you are clear you want to say no, there are six variations from which to choose.

GUIDELINES FOR SAYING NO

The word "no" gets a bad rap. We associate it with being denied something we enjoy or find pleasurable: dessert, dating a certain person, a trip, a new piece of clothing, and so on. As adults, saying no is essential to managing our lives. "No" allows us to turn down an item, task, or commitment that would rob us of time, money, sanity, health, or a number of other things that we value. "No" is a word we need to befriend! Phrase your "no" in any way that is natural for you and appropriate for the situation. Be sure you don't add "I'm sorry," because it makes you sound apologetic and weakens your "no."

1. JUST PLAIN NO
    - *"No, I'm not able to do that."*
    - *"No, I'm not willing to do that."*
    - *"No, I don't want to do that."*

2. NO, with a SHORT "BECAUSE"
    - *"No, I don't want to go to a movie, because I'm tired and need to get to bed early tonight."*
    - *"No, I won't be able to do that analysis, because we don't have those figures on hand, and it would take weeks to assemble them."*

3. PARTIAL NO
    - *"No, I won't be able to do A or B, but I can do C."*
    - *"No, I won't be able to do the Pierce or Fenner analysis, but I can do one for Smith."*

4. NOT NOW NO
    - *"No, I'm not able to do that now. I'm in the middle of the quarterly report for Randy. I will be able to get that to you by Wednesday afternoon."*

5. YES—BUT NO
    - *"Yes—but I can only help with the fundraiser until noon, then I have another appointment."*

Variation: *I can/will; however...*

The "Partial No," "Not Now No," and "Yes—But No" are useful tools to help you negotiate an amicable settlement. These techniques are also useful in deterring what could descend into an angry encounter. You are obliging the person by giving her some of what she wants. It's difficult for someone to get angry when you agree to meet a portion of her request.

6.   EMPATHETIC NO

When the other person is upset, emotional, or stressed, you may want to use an "empathetic listening statement" before saying no. If you are someone who is naturally empathetic and sensitive to disharmony, this will make it easier for you, as well.

Simply acknowledge the person's desire or need or dilemma and state that you wish you were able to comply. YOU DON'T HAVE TO DO ANYTHING TANGIBLE. Just by taking the time and energy to put yourself in the other person's shoes, you're showing care and respect.

- *"I can see you really want to go to that movie and I wish I were up for it, but I'm really tired and need to get to bed early tonight."*

- *"I can see that you are really in a bind and I wish I could help you out, but my back is to the wall with my own project."*

   Variations: *"I can tell..."; "I know...";
   "I understand..."*

The advantage of the empathetic statement is that by restating the person's problem, you buy yourself time to frame a response. Words of understanding often will head off a dispute or angry words.

Avoid using the word "should" in an empathetic no. This word is like a form of "I'm sorry." It presents an action that you are unable, unwilling, or uninterested in doing. For example, don't tell your neighbor you "should" help her with her yard sale but can't because you've got carpool. Instead, tell her: "I know you need help with your yard sale, but unfortunately I'm already booked with carpool."

"Should" is not appropriate when talking about feelings. No one really "should" feel a certain way or not. Feelings just *are,* so don't add extra guilt to your burdens, especially when the feeling you feel is unpleasant. Don't apologize for feelings that allow you to turn down requests; silently celebrate them.

Knowing the six ways to say no makes it easier to turn down or modify requests. These assertive lines cover nearly all situations except the most challenging one of all: the person who won't take "no" for an answer. Unfortunately, most of us number a few of these among our friends or relatives. And all of us have to cope with the super salesman, either in person or on the phone, who makes a specialty of never accepting no for an answer. Happily, there is one fail-safe method for dealing with these deadly people. It's called the persistent response, or more vividly, the Broken Record.

BROKEN RECORD GUIDELINES

According to Manuel Smith, Ph.D., the author of *When I Say No I Feel Guilty,* the first thing to learn in being assertive is perseverance. "One of the most important aspects of being verbally assertive is to be persistent and to keep saying what you want over and over again without getting angry, irritated, or loud," he states.[18] Dr. Smith points out that non-assertive people often lose out in conflict situations simply because they give up much too easily. They give up after the first or second no. When asking for what they want, they are too quick to give in when others give them "reasons" for not doing it. The following

guidelines are adapted from a technique that Dr. Smith and his colleague developed, called "Broken Record." It is your passport to never being snookered again.

BROKEN RECORD GUIDELINES

1. **PICK ONE SHORT SIMPLE PHRASE** about what you want or don't want. Then keep repeating it, with only minor variation, in a calm, repetitive voice until the person goes along with your request or stops his demands. For example: "I want another countertop installed—this is not the color I ordered"; "I don't want to buy the extra picture, I only want this one"; "I want to cancel this credit card"; "I'm not interested"; "That won't work for me" or "I'm not comfortable with that— and I'm not willing to do it."

2. **DON'T GET SIDETRACKED** by his questions or statements—don't answer or respond to them. Just stick to your original phrase or remain silent. When first learning broken record, expect to feel acutely uncomfortable not responding to all the questions, statements, and requests put to you. This is exactly what a master salesman or manipulative friend or family member is counting on. (See the Suspended Response, p. 74.) You don't have to run to the fire every time you hear the sirens!

3. **HANG IN THERE.** Don't stop until you have made your response just one more time than the other person. That is your only goal. If the other person makes two statements, you make three. If he makes seven, you make eight. Usually, the other person gives up after three or four times as he realizes you are not going to budge.

Example:
Someone Wants to Make Their Crisis Yours

Colleague:	I have to meet with you this afternoon.
You:	I'm not able to do that.
Colleague:	It's urgent we meet, I'm on deadline.
You:	I'm straight out and I won't be able to do that.
Colleague:	It will only take fifteen minutes of your time.
You:	I can't do it.
Colleague:	Puhlease, I'm going to be in hot water unless I complete this report.
You:	I wish I could, but I really can't.

Usually, the person making a request will get the point and stop entreating you.

The moral here is: Don't place yourself in a bind just because a colleague or friend is in one. Their crisis is not of your making; consequently, you are not compelled to make it an emergency or inconvenience for you.

Example:
Rising Above Guilt Induction and Anger

You:	I can't go shopping with you Thursday evening, because I've reserved the time to prepare the agenda and materials for Friday's meeting.
Friend:	Ohhh, preparing the agenda doesn't take any time at all. I'll help you after we finish shopping.
You:	I just can't go shopping with you Thursday evening.
Friend:	I really need your help to select a gift for John. It won't take any time at all.
You:	I can't go shopping, because I've got the agenda to do.
Friend:	I gave up my time last week to show you how to design a spread sheet, can't you just do this for me?
You:	No, I simply can't go Thursday.
Friend:	You know, I do a lot for you and it really ticks me off that you won't do this little thing for me.
You:	Look, I wish I could help you with this, because you definitely do a lot for me, but I've got to work Thursday evening.

Example:
A Friend Wants to Party

Friend:	Come on, let's go party! It's still early!
You:	I have to get up early tomorrow. I can't go party, because I need to go to bed in a little bit.
Friend:	What? Oh, come on, it's only 9 o'clock.
You:	Yes. Right about the time I need to go to bed so I can get up early tomorrow.
Friend:	You know I've heard that staying up past your bedtime helps you sleep better.
You:	Whatever. I'm going to bed in a little bit, so going out is out.
Friend:	Oh come on, it'll be fun.
You	I'm sure it would be if I didn't have to get up tomorrow. I'm going to bed in a little bit. Good night.

It's difficult to turn down the request of a friend, colleague, boss, or spouse. The person who knows you well also knows how to manipulate you by laying on guilt and in some cases by displaying anger. You have to be strong and persist in saying no, regardless of the emotional state of the person making the request. Guilt and anger are tools people use to get their way. Stick to your position. The person making the request will eventually get over being angry. By giving in, you signal your

vulnerability, and that person will use these tools again and again to get you to do what you don't want to do. The broken record technique is your best shield against manipulative anger and guilt. Use it again and again and again. It will eventually stop a vicious cycle of guilty persuasion.

To round out your limit-setting skills, there are two all-purpose statements that need to be indelibly etched into your memory.

■ **"That won't work for me."**
■ **"I'm not comfortable with that."**

These two statements are amazingly versatile and work in a wide variety of situations. Keep them ready on the tip of your tongue, and you will be able to instantly set limits without sounding abrupt or defensive.

Examples:

Friend:	I'm in the neighborhood and thought I would drop by in a few minutes.
You:	I wish we could get together, but that won't work for me.
Mate:	If Sam calls back tell him you forgot to give me his message.
You:	I'm not comfortable with that (and I'm not willing to do it).

| Colleague: | I'll get the material together for the Rogers account and you assemble the material for Simpson's. |
| You: | That won't work for me. |

| Sister: | Let's not tell the others that Dad is in the hospital right now. |
| You: | I'm not comfortable with that (and I'm not willing to do it). |

In cases like the first example, that's all that needs to be said. In other cases, you will go on to negotiate an arrangement that you *will* find comfortable or that *will* work for you.

Fielding Rude Questions

We've all been on the receiving end of questions or comments that are totally inappropriate or intrusive. Most of us either answer automatically, and later kick ourselves for doing so, or we are stunned into silence. Silence is often exactly the right response. It's one of three rejoinders that keep you from being at the mercy of people who are behaving in an ignorant, aggressive, or insensitive way. Sometimes this behavior is a momentary slip from an ordinarily civilized person, but it can also be the standard operating style of a steamroller or a manipulator. In any case, the principle of mindfulness is paramount in handling such situations because being on automatic pilot leaves you vulnerable. Your mindful response will either shut down the manipulator or remind the otherwise considerate offender that they have slipped into territory that is none of their business.

Besides remaining silent, you can answer with your own

tactical question, "Why do you ask?" Or you can give a non-answer: a pleasant but tangential statement that doesn't really answer the presumptuous question. For counteracting rude, hostile, or boorish comments, nothing can beat a civilized rejoinder following quickly on the heels of an rude remark. You get your point across without being embarrassed or reduced to outrage, finger pointing, or moralizing. You retain the high ground, which is precisely the ground you want for your own.

Following are the three strategies. As you warm to the task of backing down rude people, you will most certainly come up with your own creative variations.

SILENCE

Here are some examples of questions and comments that are best handled by remaining silent.

- Have you put on some weight recently?
- You look awfully tired.
- Are you pregnant?
- You shouldn't wear that color.
- What caused your divorce?

Silence in the face of extreme rudeness is solid gold. For maximum effect, it should be accompanied by strong eye contact signaling that you have heard the comment and choose not to respond. When you remain silent, any but the most insensitive or hostile person will get the message and go on to another topic. For the occasional boor who persists, your civilized—and assertive—response should be, "I'm not comfortable answering that question."

THE TACTICAL QUESTION: "WHY DO YOU ASK?"

Here are some examples of rude questions that can be handled well with the tactical question, "Why do you ask?"

- What did you pay for that jacket?
- Have you had a face lift?
- How old are you?
- Is that ring real gold?
- How much do you make?

Calmly inquiring, "Why do you ask?" gives you time to mindfully decide how you wish to continue. It is critical that you ask in a pleasant and well-modulated voice, without the slightest hint of hostility or sarcasm. Think automated-voice-messaging-with-warmth. Your question will jog most people into realizing that their question is inappropriate, and they will mutter something like, "Oh, sorry —shouldn't have asked." For hard-core boors who persist with their questioning, your response is, once again, "I'm not comfortable answering that question."

THE NON-ANSWER

Here is an amusing alternative to silence and the tactical question.

Rude Question
What did you pay for that jacket?
Civilized Rejoinder
Oh, it was a steal at twice the price!

Uncouth Question
Have you had a face life?
Civilized Rejoinder
Wow, do I look that good? Aren't you kind!

Uncouth Question
How old are you?
Civilized Rejoinder
It's wonderful how little age matters these days—it's really about how you feel!

Rude Question
> Is that ring real gold?

Civilized Rejoinder
> I'm so glad you like it.

Rude Question
> How much do you make?

Civilized Rejoinder
> Enough to pay the bills and keep me happy, I can assure you!

These civilized rejoinders make it clear that you have heard the other person and have chosen not to answer. Similarly, your reply can take the conversation into a new and more comfortable direction. Either way, you have asserted your right not to answer an intrusive question, all the while remaining calm and pleasant.

TEN

Assert

> "Lying is done with words,
>
> but also with silence."
>
> – Adrianne Rich

ere are three crucial aspects of assertive speaking that women will need to master in order to make their language more effective and powerful.

- Ask directly for what you want
- Deliver "I" messages
- Ask for feedback, clarification, and cooperation

ASKING DIRECTLY FOR WHAT YOU NEED AND WANT

In fifth grade, when I was a reporter on the school newspaper, I learned the essentials of getting a story in short order. That was a valuable communication lesson that I've used in some form or another ever since. It is a very efficient framework

for asking directly for what you want. The five "W"s of reporting (Who, What, When, Where & Why) are key to making a clear, assertive request.

1. Focus directly and exclusively on your request.
   - Avoid irrelevant detail
   - Stick to the point
   - Don't add personal comments or associations

2. Use sentence frames that include specific and concrete information stating

   WHAT

   WHEN

   WHY

   I want _____ *by* _____ *because* _____ .

   I need _____ *by* _____ *because* _____ .

   I'd like you to _____ *by* _____ *because* _____ .

   "*I want the Fisher data by Thursday because Sam is coming on Monday to review all the accounts.*"

   "*I need the proofed copy by Wednesday in order to drop it by the printer on my way into work Thursday.*"

   "*I'd like you to finish the Dawson project by the 12th because I need to include it in this month's report to New York.*"

   "*I need you to fix dinner Thursday night because I'll be at my CA class and won't be home 'til later.*"

It is important that your nonverbal behavior matches your message so that you are not sending mixed signals. Many women are uncomfortable when they have to make any kind of request and try to soften it by being tentative about what they want and when. This isn't civilized, it's simply confusing. If your request is urgent, don't sound or look uncertain or nonchalant. If the issue is serious, don't smile or make light of your request.

DELIVERING "I" MESSAGES

The "I" message is one of your most valuable communication techniques. It enables you to speak up in an honest and objective manner and keeps you from being unduly emotional. By using "I" messages, you automatically take responsibility for your own feelings. In addition, delivering "I" messages keeps you from using loaded words that elicit defensiveness in others. The way you phrase an "I" message guarantees that your opinions, requests, or objections are neither critical nor defensive.

Psychologist Dr. Thomas Gordon and his wife, sociologist Linda Adams, have developed four levels of assertive messages.[19] These are civilized and self-respecting ways to speak up and out and ask for what you want.

1. **Disclosing "I" Message.** A straightforward comment about what you think, feel, or believe. It can be either positive or negative. You clearly state your opinion without permission, qualification, or apology.

   Examples: "I like the way this room is decorated."
   "I enjoy working on this project with you."
   "I get upset when you criticize me in front of other people."

2. **Preventive "I" Message.** When you have a clear need, and to get it met you must involve another person, you directly ask for what you want. It is called preventive because it avoids the potential conflict and disappointment

inherent in thinking that someone else should know what you need or want, or the misunderstandings that arise when requests are delivered indirectly or tentatively.

Examples: "I need your help in cleaning the apartment."
"I want to take our vacation in Hawaii this year."
"I need your help getting this report out."

> **"My heart was racing but I felt OK because I knew that I wouldn't have to take back anything I said."**
>
> – Marie
> when she first used an "I" message to stand up to an obnoxious co-worker

3. **Responsive "I" Message.** When someone requests something that will take your time, money, or energy, you take full responsibility for the decision to comply or not comply. By employing the personal check (discussed in Chapter Six) before responding, you are able to say no without excuse or apology or placing the responsibility on someone else or some outside force.

Examples: "No, I don't want to do that."
"No, I'm not willing to do that."
"No, I'm not able to do that."

You may, however, want to describe the effect that complying with their request would have on you.

"No, I can't meet with you now because I have to complete the sales report."

4. **Three-Part "I" Message.** When your needs or rights have been infringed upon, you deliver a forthright "I" message that:
   1) describes the behavior of concern;
   2) expresses how you feel about it;
   3) describes the tangible effects of the behavior.

   It keeps you specifically focused on the behavior that you find unpleasant, uncomfortable, or damaging.

   Example: "When you don't call to tell me you're running late, I feel irritated/annoyed/angry because I could have used the time to finish up the report I was working on."

The major point of the three-part message is to describe how the other person's behavior is affecting you. If I want you to change your behavior, it certainly helps if I give you a convincing reason to change. The research in this area suggests that concrete and tangible effects are the most persuasive reasons.[20]

Six common and concrete effects are:
1. Costs money
2. Harms possessions
3. Consumes time
4. Interferes with effective work relationships
5. Causes extra work
6. Harms personal relationships

Using the following sentence frame to deliver a three-part message makes it relatively easy to do. It may seem stilted at first, but with practice it will sound more natural. The "I" message keeps you from being accusatory or judgmental.

> When you _____
> I feel _____
> Because _____

HERE'S HOW IT WORKS

Scene at home:

"When you have a snack and leave the food and dishes on the counter... I feel irritated...
Because I have to clean that up before I can start dinner."

This is a clean non-judgmental statement that is absolutely specific about what behavior is causing the problem (leaving the food and dishes out). Although it may take an uncommonly strong act of will, it's crucial to the effectiveness of the message not to ruin it with a judgmental dig *("When you're too lazy to clean up after yourself"* or *"When you don't do your fair share")*.

Scene at the office:

"When you took the credit for coming up with the new promotion idea... I was angry...
Because it was my idea, and I spent a great deal of time developing it."

Again, this is a clean, strong, focused statement about what behavior caused the problem (taking credit for the idea), how you feel about it, and the effects of the behavior. It is important to refrain from the very human urge to be sarcastic, blaming, or moralistic *("Thanks a lot for using my idea!" "You've ruined my work!" "You had no right to...")*.

ASKING FOR CLARIFICATION, FEEDBACK, AND COOPERATION

Often, the occasion when it is particularly important to be assertive is the very time you are stressed and unsure of what to say. Here are some Assertive Sentences that are appropriate, non-threatening, and keep the conversation productive and civilized.

1. **How to Ask for Clarification (Use Active Listening)**
    "I want to make sure I understand you. Are you saying...."
    (Then paraphrase information)
    "It seems that I'm not completely aware of what's going on. Can you clarify the situation for me?"
    (Then paraphrase information)
    "I'm not clear about how this will work... will you go over it again please?"
    (Then paraphrase information)
    "I'm uncertain about what it is you're planning to do (how this would work, what the gains are here, etc.) Could you clear this up for me?"
    (Then paraphrase information)

2. **How to Ask for Feedback to Improve Performance and/or Defuse Criticism**
    "What am I doing that makes me just average on this performance rating?"
    "Could you give me some specific example of ways I could improve?"
    "What is it about the way I did___ that you don't like?"
    (negative inquiry)
    "I want to explain my reasons for____. Can you give me a few minutes to do that?"
    "I can see how you might have been disappointed in my report." (fogging) *"What are the main things you think I could have done differently?"*

Fogging is a technique that allows you to handle criticism without being defensive, by making a noncommittal statement such as "You could be right about that," "I can see how it might seem that way," "Perhaps I should have done it that way." The statement acknowledges the other's point of view without actually agreeing or disagreeing.

Fogging Statements
> *You could be right about that.*
> *You're probably right about that.*
> *You might be right about that.*
> *I can see how it might seem that way.*
> *Maybe that would work better.*
> *It does look that way.*
> *Perhaps it would work better that way.*

3. **How to Ask for Cooperation**

   a. To Affirm the Relationship
   > *"Our relationship is important to me, and I want to work this out. Are you willing to work on it?"*
   > *"I want to discuss this problem because I think it is having a bad effect on our relationship. When can we get together?"*

   b. For Mutual Problem-Solving
   > *"What's the best way for us to get this project done?"*
   > *"Will you help me brainstorm some ways we can solve this problem?"*

   c. To Cope with Resistance
   > *"If you are not willing to work out this agreement, what is your suggestion as to how we can solve this problem?"*

"If this solution doesn't work for you, what would?"

"I want to work this out with you. Do you want to work it out?"

(In response to hostile "yessing") *"I get the feeling that you are saying yes only to humor me. Is that so?"*

"I would like to create a climate between us where we can talk about what is going on. Do you have some ideas about how to do that?"

Five Steps to Assertive Habits

STEP 1. OBSERVE: When you consciously realize a particular behavior isn't in your best interest, start observing its negative consequences.

STEP 2. CHOOSE: Mindfully choose a healthier new behavior to put in its place.

STEP 3. PRACTICE: Anticipate when you can practice using the new behavior. Use it as often as possible in the early stage.

- Know that your first attempts may be bumbling and partial.

- In this early stage you will often catch yourself behaving in the old way.

IT IS IMPORTANT not to give in to the old habitual pattern. Go ahead and conspicuously override the old behavior with the new behavior. Override it even if it means contradicting yourself, looking and/or feeling foolish, or even reneging on a commitment. ("As I've thought it through, I see I can't…" "I've reconsidered what I said, and…" "On sober thought…" "I'm afraid I was a little premature….")

STEP 4. INTEGRATE: After some practice, the new behavior may still seem a bit foreign but will, on balance, be satisfying.

- Deliberately observe and be mindful of your progress.

- Commend and reward yourself.

STEP 5. MONITOR: Finally, the new behavior will become well established and semi-automatic.

- Watch out for high stress times.

- Forgive yourself an occasional lapse.

A major barrier to changing bad habits is thinking that they are eliminated through acts of will. Bad habits and compulsions are rarely conquered by determined resolutions or ordering ourselves not to go on doing this or that.

Stop trying to use force. When you push and force others, you get a reaction. The law of physical reciprocity states that for each action there is an equal and opposing reaction. There is a similar rule of psychological reciprocity, and that same dynamic is at work when you try to push and force yourself.

The only effective way to get rid of bad habits is to substitute the positive for the negative: the "I will" for "I won't." That negative thought or bad habit does not belong to you. Turn it loose and let it go. Then quickly bring in another more positive thought or action to fill its place. The process is just like the childhood game of musical chairs. You put the new healthy thought or action in the place of the old. When the bad habit or the negative thought comes back in your mind, it will have no place to sit.

NOTES

Negotiate

Whether we identify it or not, we are negotiating all of the time. With whom? Bosses, peers, subordinates, customers, clients, vendors, spouses, children, friends, lovers, in-laws, even our pets! For what? Salary, budgets, space, goods, perks, power, decisions, choices, autonomy, consideration, respect, and desirable changes in behavior. Most of what we negotiate about can be measured in terms of time and energy, money and self-esteem. Routinely using the personal checks (Chapter 6) keeps you clear about the personal costs of your commitments.

At heart, negotiating is a very simple process. In everyday situations it often involves nothing more than saying, "I would like to do…" "What would you like to do?" or "I need…" "What do you need?" or "This would work for me, would it work for you?" This is the sort of "invisible" negotiation that

goes on all the time as we choose things to do with a friend or divide up tasks with a spouse or a colleague at work. There is a goal—making some new arrangements or finding a solution to a current predicament—but the process is natural and non-defensive. We discuss, analyze, confer, brainstorm, and consider various solutions without anxiety or self-consciousness. Often we are not even aware that we are in fact negotiating—we're simply having a purposeful conversation.

Negotiations tend to make us self-conscious when conflicts of interests or opinions surface, or when there are high stakes for limited resources. Frequently, people become reflexively defensive and assume a competitive negotiating stance. For everyday negotiation, we are able to argue dispassionately based on the merits of the situation. In competitive negotiation, we tend to lock into a position and then vehemently defend it with our minds closed to other options. When we focus only on our position, the idea of balancing mutual interests goes out the window.

This competitive (win/lose) approach is quicker and easier in the short run but much less effective than the collaborative (win/win) approach in the long run. These two universal negotiating approaches, collaborative and competitive, are so ingrained that we pay little attention to our choice when we are involved in the process. The key to everyday negotiations is to mindfully choose to avoid the competitive approach. We need to concentrate on using our natural collaborative conversation style, as well as the other three Assertive Communication skills: **Listen, Limit** and **Assert.**

Effective negotiation requires balance. Balance in the face of conflict requires the honesty to acknowledge when we are the ones seeking the upper hand and the candor to speak out when the other side is getting greedy. By saying *"This is out of balance—this needs to work for both of us,"* we are more likely to find solutions that are mutually acceptable.

As women, we're afraid of confrontation because we are

trained to do what's nice rather than what's fair or what's just. We have to realize, though, that sorting out problems through assertive confrontation often clears the air and strengthens a relationship. Fortunately, women's communication style is rooted in empathy and negotiation. While all those boys were playing rough-and-tumble "I'm first, you're last" games, girls were negotiating and cooperating: "You get the tea set and I'll get the cookies." "I should get the tea set because it's mine." "Hey, let's use my tea set instead—it's bigger and has enough cups for all of us!" With the courage to stand up for ourselves and the sureness of our abilities and limits, negotiation can be the easiest part of assertiveness.

Negotiation is the self-respecting way to address constructively any ongoing situations that interfere with your work, well-being, or happiness. It can be applied to a partner who frequently leaves a mess in the kitchen, an aggressive co-worker, a mate who often criticizes, or any other situation that is a significant problem for you.

THREE STEPS TO NEGOTIATING

STEP 1

- Introduce the idea on a positive note and make a strong statement about how important the matter is to you

- Speak assertively, stating your opinions, feelings, and needs calmly and respectfully

- Deliver an "I" Message

Example:

"I'd like to discuss something that's been bothering me a lot. I need to work this out because our relationship is important to me and right now I'm worried about it.

When you criticize me in front of your family, I feel betrayed because I count on you to support me."

STEP 2

■ Listen actively to the other's point of view.

Example:

Mate: *"You're too sensitive. My family likes to kid and joke around with each other, and that's what I was doing with you. Lighten up."*

You: *"So you criticize just as a joke and don't really mean anything by it. And you think I'm too sensitive because it hurts my feelings."*

STEP 3

■ Use a problem-solving approach to negotiate a fair resolution of the undesirable situation.

Example:

"Yes, you're right, I am a sensitive person. Since I am upset by criticism even if you are joking, let's figure out how we can kid around without me feeling put-down."

These three steps, using the basic skills of Civilized Assertiveness, allow you to remain respectful, mindful, and balanced throughout the encounter. Using this framework keeps you focused on the current problem. It is imperative to a successful negotiation that you avoid blaming, shaming, or bringing up past sins.

Dishing out a laundry list of the other person's shortcomings will only cause them to become defensive and possibly shoot insults back at you. This is not the kind of interaction you want! Instead, use the above framework and non-judgmental and unemotional words to get your point across. It also helps when you are clear on what you want out of the negotiation.

> ## Successful Negotiation = A Clear Purpose
>
> Two Fundamental Reasons to Ask for Change
>
> ⁕ To improve or maintain productivity
>
> ⁕ To guard or maintain the relationship
>
> Whenever you ask for a change in behavior, you need to be able to tie your request to one or both of these reasons. Requesting change ultimately needs to be in the service of the job or in the service of the relationship.

Civilized Assertiveness in Action

The two examples that follow show how the negotiation process works. The beauty of using this approach is that it keeps the conversation focused. It keeps you from getting sidetracked into discussing irrelevant issues or becoming contentious.

It is essential to this type of interaction that you are very clear about the ultimate purpose of the negotiation. In both cases demonstrated below—working out areas of responsibility for household chores and confronting a husband's frequent put downs—the purpose is to reduce friction in order to guard or enhance the personal relationship.

NEGOTIATING FOR A CLEANER KITCHEN

Jack and Jill have been married for five years and in general are good about sharing tasks and taking equal responsibility for running the house. However, Jack frequently leaves a mess in the kitchen, inconveniencing Jill, who usually prepares dinner. This is an example of a relatively minor problem. Nonetheless, it is important to confront this situation because it has become a source of stress in the relationship. Everyday negotiation would go something like this:

Jill:	Jack, I'd like to discuss something that's been bothering me and I think it's causing some friction in our relationship.	*Introducing the problem without blame.*
	When you leave a mess in the kitchen, I get angry because I have to clean it up before I can fix dinner.	*A clear three-part "I" statement that minimizes the chances of Jack becoming defensive.*
Jack:	The dishwasher is always full so I can't put the dirty dishes in.	
Jill:	You're right, we really do leave the dishwasher full with a lot of stuff a lot of the time.	*Active listening that acknowledges the important aspect of the situation that Jack has put forth.*
Jack:	I usually clear things away when I can get them in.	
Jill:	So, when the dishwasher is full, you would have to unload it	*More active listening to acknowledge further elements of the problem.*

before you could clean things up. Is this the main problem?

Jack: Yes.

Jill: O.K., so let's try to figure out a system for unloading the dishwasher more often. Do you have any ideas?

Starts the negotiation to find a mutually acceptable solution to the problem.

Jack: No... not really, it's not that big a deal.

Downplays and avoids the problem.

Jill: Maybe it's not that big a deal, but it has been bothering me, and I think it is becoming a problem.

Does some fogging and then restates the problem (broken record).

Jack: I don't think there's a real problem here.

Continues to down play the problem.

Jill: O.K., so we see this differently. It is a real problem for me. I need you to work this out with me.

Jack: O.K., if it's that important to you.

Jill: Thanks—it really is. One thing that might help is if you would run the dishwasher before you go to bed, I could unload it every morning

Jill might be tempted to give up at this point— after all, she's talking about dirty dishes, not world peace. Fortunately, she has thought things through and has done the math: dirty dishes x 365. That's a real problem!

Offers a possible solution.

when I'm having my
second cup of coffee.
Would you be willing to
run it every night? That
way both of us could
clean up as we go along.

Jack: Actually, I think it   *Counter offer from*
       would be better if you   *Jack that is acceptable.*
       ran it at night. I could
       unload it   in the
       morning while waiting
       for the coffee to perk.

Jill: Great, let's see how that
       works.

Perhaps a one-time direct and open confrontation of a problem, such as the example above, is enough to change the situation. Both people involved learn that touchy situations can be discussed openly. They also see that through a little negotiation, problems stressing the relationship can be solved. However, change takes time, and usually you will be tested to see if you really meant it.

It may take several tries to come up with a solution that really works, but using this approach makes it easy to reopen the discussion and go back to the drawing board if necessary. Too often people are loath to confront issues because they are afraid of endangering the relationship or causing more friction. Far from endangering the relationship, this type of non-defensive confrontation actually strengthens it. When a problem has been successfully worked through, invariably both people feel better about the situation, about themselves, and about each other.

NEGOTIATING FOR RESPECTFUL TREATMENT

Christine is at her wit's end with her husband, David. They are both college-educated professionals with good careers, but he constantly runs her down in front of other people. He makes comments like, "I can't believe you got an MBA" and tells people about the "stupid" things she does. His criticisms seem to be aimed toward changing her, and she keeps trying to accommodate him by doing things the way he tells her to do. Recently, she has felt sad and angry about his attacks and his demands for changes in her habits and behavior. She knows deep down it's time for a major change.

Christine:	David, I need to talk to you about something that's really been bothering me for a long time, and I think it's damaging our relationship. When you insult me in front of other people, I feel betrayed because you're my husband and I need you on my side.	*Three-part "I" message*
David:	What are you talking about? Puh-leeze, I don't insult you.	*Deflection/denial of a problem*
Christine:	David, remember the Wegmans' party last week? You told a whole roomful of people that I "wasn't fit to drive a car because I'm such a space cadet."	*Responding to the amount of truth in his statement by providing a specific example*

David: Oh, there were only,
            like, two people
            listening. Besides, it's
            just a joke. And you
            know how scary you
            can be behind the
            wheel.

Christine: It doesn't matter how   *Refocusing the*
            many people were   *discussion*
            listening, David—I
            heard it. Maybe I'm
            not the best driver, but   *Fogging*
            having my abilities run   *Broken Record*
            down by my life
            partner is hurtful to
            me, and I'm asking
            you to stop.

David: Aw, for Pete's sake,
            Christine! I was just
            kidding around.

Christine: So when you say   *Active listening*
            things that zing me to
            other people, you're
            just trying to make a
            joke.

David: Yeah! Man, don't get
            so uptight about it!

Christine: Well, David, I am   *"I" statement about*
            uptight about it. I'm   *feelings*
            sensitive about this,   *Broken Record*
            and I'm asking you to
            stop.

David: Yeah yeah yeah, okay.
            I'll stop if you're
            gonna make such a big
            deal out of it.

Christine: David, I get the feeling   *Active Listening*
            you're just saying yes
            to me so this
            conversation will end.
            Is that true?

David: [sighs heavily] Look,
            Christine, this is just
            ridiculous. One little
            comment and you're in
            orbit about this. Relax!

Christine: So you think that I'm   *Active Listening to get*
            taking this picking at   *clarification*
            me thing too seriously?

David: I'm not "picking" at
            you! I'm just making a
            joke.

Christine: David, you have a   *Positive reinforcement*
            great sense of humor,
            but I feel betrayed by   *Assert*
            you when the joke is at
            my expense. I'm asking
            you to stop. Your jokes   *Request for change and*
            hurt me and it's   *statement of how the*
            putting a rift between   *behavior affects her*
            us. I need you to be on
            my side, to support
            me. Are you willing to
            do that for me?

David: Yeah...yeah, I guess so.

Christine: Thanks, David. That's   *Positive reinforcement*
            one of the things I love
            about you, your
            willingness to work
            things out. So, how   *Negotiation*
            about we come up
            with a signal I can give
            you in case you say
            something that zings
            me in front of other
            people? Like, I stroke
            my chin?

Christine doesn't back down, despite the fact that David's comments could guilt her into silence by insinuating that she's "sensitive" or that her complaint is "ridiculous." Christine doesn't buy it and holds the line on how David's behavior hurts her. She lets him know how she feels and how this situation is affecting their relationship. She then asks him if he's willing to work on this with her, and then she tries to figure out a subtle solution for the problem (the chin-stroking) that will help the problem but not embarrass David in front of others (like openly calling him on the insults).

This exchange will likely not be the end of the problem—David's behavior has become a habit—so there will be more conversations about David's verbal abuse of Christine. The good news is that each discussion will either strengthen their relationship and bring them closer, or necessitate Christine having to reassess the total relationship in light of his desire (or inability) to change his destructive behavior.

For very difficult situations you will need to plan ahead by outlining and clarifying the problem. It is important to take time to plan and prepare before confronting the situation with the

other person. The worksheet at the end of this chapter is designed to focus your thinking by getting essential information down on paper. It helps you clearly articulate what is bothering you, why you are bothered, and what specifically you want to change.

CLARIFY THE PROBLEM, BRAINSTORM ALTERNATIVES, AND REHEARSE

After you have outlined the problem using the worksheet on the following page, talk over the situation with several people whose judgment you respect. Someone not involved in the situation can see it more clearly and objectively. Ask for help to define the problem and develop some alternatives for dealing with it. Then script yourself along the lines of the negotiation scenarios in this chapter. For added confidence, rehearse the negotiation with a friend, and have her throw you as many curveballs as possible. If you can't readily respond, brainstorm some new phrases and rehearse them until you are as comfortable as you are likely to get.

CIVILIZED ASSERTIVENESS® WORKSHEET

1. Briefly, what is the situation?

2. Describe the behavior you want changed:
   a. Specifically, what is this person doing now?

   b. Specifically, what do you want him/her to do?

3. Review past history:
   a. What have you said regarding this behavior in the past?

   b. What do you do instead of asserting yourself?

   c. Why do you want to start asserting yourself now?

   d. Which of your assertive rights are being violated? (See Chapter 4)

4. List three positive characteristics of this person.

5. What is your major goal for this negotiation?

6. What is your fall-back plan if you do not accomplish your goal?

Assertive Salary Negotiations

Salary negotiation is by definition a high-stakes ordeal and particularly intimidating to most women.

Why?

Because a number of women are uncomfortable tooting their own horn, reciting their accomplishments, and touting their successes. It seems...well, unseemly. But if we are to close that 23-cents-on-the-dollar pay gap, we need to come across as competent and as valuable as men. *They* have no such aversions to advertising their superior performance. From early childhood on, most men have been skillfully trumpeting their accomplishments—both real and imagined.

Some of us will never be comfortable with the bold braggadocio that seems effortless for many men—but it is imperative that we consistently and mindfully discuss our accomplishments and advertise our successes.

Lifelong Job Description
Duty #1: I will be my own PR agent.

Today, right this minute, mentally write those seven words into your lifelong job description. And add: I will keep those above me in the organization—those responsible for setting salaries, bestowing perks and handing out our job responsibilities—informed and up to date on my major accomplishments and successes.

Know that the powers that be aren't mind readers; they have people and responsibilities pressing in from all sides. You are competing with well-orchestrated advertising campaigns from others in your organization—this is no time to hide your light!

I have been told by a number of career counselors that men frequently discuss their jobs as if they run the company. However, women often discuss their jobs as if they are several notches below their actual position. Even more damaging to their careers is that for many women it amounts to a taboo to brag about their work.

Well, my dears—get over it!

Bragging is exactly what you need to do, particularly when you are making a case for why you should get a raise. Take heart—there are civilized ways to do this. But it must be done, because if you are reticent or feel awkward talking about your accomplishments, you will end up sounding vague or unconvinced of your own worth. A good strategy is to pick three or four succinct points about yourself and relate each directly to a criterion for promotion. (See the Personal Job Inventory at the end of this chapter.) I've never been particularly comfortable trumpeting my accomplishments and talents. However, I am

good at speaking enthusiastically and persuasively about projects I feel are worthwhile or that have challenged me. I love discussing them and am quite comfortable and not at all self-conscious about it. A wise counselor and friend once said, "Don't get too personally involved in your own life," and I've found that to be a big help in the work arena. Practicing a bit of detachment and conscientiously trying to imagine how your accomplishments and performance look to others is a valuable experience. It helps you become a more articulate, astute agent for yourself.

Money is an emotionally loaded issue for many of us, and there are a couple of issues that hamper women in particular. First, a number of employment specialists say that women often fail to put themselves in their bosses' positions when making a request. Instead, they focus on their needs rather than the needs of the organization. Again, a bit of detachment and perspective-taking are essential. Second, for numerous reasons, women are much more likely to have money phobias.

> " Men often use money as their only measurement of success while women tend to embrace anything but money as a definition of success. Women need to learn that it's OK to include money as yet another valid goal and definition of success. "
>
> – Pam Dumonceau
> Financial Advisor, Consistent Values, Inc.
> Denver, Colorado

We negotiate all the time in all sorts of situations and it usually rolls along quite well. We don't think much about how we swap information and we talk in an unself-conscious way. We get in trouble when the stakes start getting high—emotionally or financially. Then we are apt to become self-conscious, which changes the process. Often, we sink into a win-lose stance. We dig in and just hold on. At that point we polarize the process and either demand that we get every bit of what we asked for or become overwhelmed and give up. Salary negotiations generally fall under the high stakes umbrella.

Not surprisingly, there is a significant gender difference in salary negotiations. Men can be more than mildly apprehensive—they can be nervous as hell—but they don't have as violent or fearful a reaction as women. Remember the preschool playground: Boys get lots of experience in being challenged, standing up for themselves, and selling themselves as superior—the essence of salary negotiation.

I have developed the following framework based on interviewing a number of executives who do salary negotiations and from the research of professional negotiators. Once again, though, I think the most useful information came from listening to hundreds of women who discussed their salary negotiations and told my workshop groups what worked and what didn't. Every situation is, of course, different for different people, but there are certain predictable themes that run through nearly all salary reviews.

There is generally a discussion of your professional and work-related duties and often of personal qualities that help (or hinder) your progress at work. These, and the overall health of the company, are the basis for the change in compensation—or lack thereof. Salary negotiation goes better when you yourself are prepared with well thought out points regarding your contributions and value to the organization.

ASSERTIVE SALARY NEGOTIATIONS

PART ONE: BACKGROUND PREPARATION

It pays to do your homework! If you think you should be paid more, you need to prove it. Be creative and be thorough.

1. **Know** *specifically* **what you want out of the negotiation.**

   Do you want a particular promotion that includes more job responsibilities, or do you simply want more money and/or greater decision-making power for what you are already doing?

2. **Determine your market value.**

   Compare your salary to what other people are paid in your own company and in other companies like yours.

   ■ Talk to friends and acquaintances who work for competitors.

   ■ Check out want ads for positions similar to yours.

   ■ You can find out what others with your comparable job description are making in your area by calling the Bureau of Labor Statistics to request salary surveys by occupation and region. In addition, most trade magazines, websites, and journals publish salary surveys annually.

3. **Assess your specific value to the organization by doing the "Personal Job Inventory" on page 121.**

   This is your objective analysis of your contributions to the organization as well as a realistic appraisal of your strengths and weaknesses. From this exercise you will target three to five of your important strengths and contributions, which you constantly weave into your negotiation.

4. **Analyze the negotiation from your boss's (the organization's) perspective.**

   Consider the organization's (your boss's) wants, needs, and concerns. Visualize a giant blackboard with a line down the middle—your needs on one side and your boss's (the organization's) needs on the other. Think through how your goals for the negotiation meet these needs or address their concerns. For example, if there is an organizational push for increased productivity, show—as specifically as you can—how many more widgets will be sold due to your promotion. Be realistic in the appraisal of the strength of your arguments.

5. **Have a fall-back plan.**

   Think through some secondary goal(s) if your primary goal(s) can't be met. For example, if a raise just isn't possible, negotiate for what you consider the next best thing(s) that would make you more satisfied with your job, such as flex time, job share, or a bonus. These options are especially helpful in economic downturns.

   Financial/Material Options
   bonus
   tuition reimbursement
   company car
   expense allowance
   an assistant

   Lifestyle Options
   flex time
   additional vacation time
   job sharing
   periodic or regular telecommuting

PART TWO: THE MEETING

■ If possible, schedule the meeting for a Tuesday, Wednesday, Thursday mid-morning or after lunch.

■ Appearance. Don't "dress up" but do choose a standard work outfit you know is becoming and comfortable and do take the extra time to be impeccably groomed.

■ Your manner should be warm and pleasant, but not overly friendly. The discussion should be businesslike, not personal. Throughout the discussion remain upbeat, positive, and respectful.

■ Regard asking for a raise as a measure of self-respect. Rarely are bosses surprised or offended that you feel you should be better paid; most give you points for it.

■ An opening statement might be: "I want you to know how much I like working here," (if you've initiated it) or "There are several reasons I think I should get a raise/salary increase/an annual bonus/ larger stock options/promotion." Then immediately go on to state the major strengths you identified in your "Personal Job Inventory."

■ Focus on your value, not your need. Don't discuss why you need the raise (high house payment, kids in college, etc.). You get a raise because you are worth it, not because you need the money.

■ Don't be too specific about how much money you want. Some professional negotiators compare the final stage of salary negotiations to a poker game: Try to get the other person to make the first move. If you are pressed to give a figure, don't. Instead, have in mind a range that reflects market value. That gives leeway for some compromise.

■ If it turns out that a raise is just not possible, be
determined to negotiate some perk that will make your
job easier or your life better. (See #5 of Background
Preparation.)

PART THREE: NEGOTIATION IS AN ONGOING PROCESS

Immediately start planning for your next salary negotiation. If you are rebuffed for any kind of raise or extended compensation, ask about a reassessment in three months, or four, or
six, or any amount of time that seems suitable. If you work in
an organization that does not do regular reviews, make an
appointment at the end of your review to discuss this again at
a set future time and date.

One caveat of salary negotiation: Realize that if you are
repeatedly turned down for raises year after year, or just given
meager compensation hikes, something is afoot. It may be that
the organization wants you to improve in some way and is afraid
to tell you. (Managers can be non-assertive, too!) You will have
to sit them down in your reviews and ask them about this yourself. It's also possible that you simply haven't improved to their
standards or that the company keeps changing their standards.
Most glaring among these, though, is the possibility that your
company simply doesn't value you that much—maybe your talents and work style don't fully mesh with their goals and objec-
tives. In that case, it's probably time to move on. Start looking
immediately—it's easier to get a job when you have a job.

Even with good evaluations and raises, it's important to
reassess yourself from time to time. Update your resume and see
what new skills you've acquired or old skills you've strengthened.
Occasionally scan the "help wanted" section of newspaper or
trade magazines and websites to see what talents and qualities are
wanted. Do the ads keep looking for experience with a certain
type of software? Perhaps now is the time to learn about it, and
you may be able to negotiate for your employer to pay for it!

Personal Job Inventory

1. What do I most enjoy doing and why?

2. How has my job description changed since I was hired?

3. How have my job responsibilities expanded since I was hired?

4. How has my job performance improved since my last salary negotiation? (In what ways am I better at my job or more productive than my peers?)

5. What specific things have benefited the organization? (Business brought in, projects handled, innovative ideas or actions, time or money saved.)

6. What do I least enjoy doing and why? What are my weaknesses on the job and what steps am I taking to correct or compensate for them?

NOTES

Criticism

We've discussed how to confront someone else's behavior, but how do you react to criticism? Giving or receiving criticism evokes emotions ranging anywhere from mild apprehension to stark terror. Often the psychological stress is accompanied by physical signs such as heart palpitations, butterflies in the stomach, and sweaty palms. Our voices are too high or too low, and we can't find the right words. Little wonder that most of us put off or avoid giving or receiving criticism as long as possible.

The more we procrastinate, the greater the risk the problem will escalate. But take heart—the skills of Civilized Assertiveness will help us cope with uncomfortable, awkward, or difficult situations.

ACCEPTING CRITICISM

In the area of accepting criticism, women can learn some valuable lessons by observing men. Through engaging in competitive sports and by receiving criticism in school (boys seven times more frequently than girls), men are socialized to accept and benefit from criticism and confront unacceptable behavior. Since girls tend to be more conforming and less confrontational, they have little experience in handling criticism. Consequently, women avoid situations where they risk being criticized and often delay confronting difficult situations.

Many of the Assertive Sentences (p. 93) are appropriate when you are on the receiving end of criticism. The goal is to react honestly and maturely without becoming defensive or apologetic. Any time you are learning new skills or taking on new challenges, you are likely to make mistakes. Remember that a fundamental assertive right is to take responsibility for mistakes.

A major roadblock to accepting criticism is the fact that sometimes the criticism is untrue, overstated, or presented in a hostile manner. In such cases women tend to get hurt and/or defensive. They often pull inside themselves and focus on how incompetent or "done in" they feel. But this is exactly the wrong thing to do. It keeps us from taking action. When you have been criticized, it is essential to direct your thoughts outward rather than inward. Here's how:[21]

Rule of Thumb for Criticism

**Match your response to the amount of truth
contained in the criticism, decide which of
the three types of criticism you are dealing with,
and then respond accordingly.**

Not True • Partially True • True

When you match your response to the amount of truth in the criticism, you neutralize the emotional content and can instead focus on the problem that's at the root of the criticism. Doing this allows you to find something objective that is to your advantage to change. At other times, the process helps you deflate angry insults and uncover the fact that they have nothing to do with you.

1. **Not true:** A criticism that is untrue, either completely or so highly distorted that it is basically untrue.

   For example:
   "You never prepare your reports correctly," when, in fact, you did only one report incorrectly, or
   "Every time we discuss this you get defensive," when you've only been defensive on two occasions.

   What to do:

   ✳ Perform an active listening paraphrase.
   "You think that I never do my reports correctly."

   ✳ Respectfully disagree.
   "I don't see it that way. I've always been proud of my reports and can only think of one that I fouled up."

   ✳ Request specifics.
   "What other report besides the Smith report have I prepared incorrectly?" (Great for deflating "never" and "always" statements.)

2. **Partially true:** A criticism that has some truth to it, but is exaggerated and/or delivered in a hostile manner.

   For example:
   "You really blew the entire presentation for the whole company," when you didn't do your best during your portion, but you only had presented a small part of the entire program.

   What to do:
   Use a fogging line (see p. 94) and then go on to balance the perception with any reasonable evidence you have.

   "I can see how you might have been disappointed by the first part of my report, but the summary was well received, and actually my portion was only a small part of the whole program."

Never apologize in response to an untrue or partially true criticism.

3. **True:** A criticism that is true, stated clearly and directly without hostility.

   For example:

   Boss: *"The main point of sending this report was to highlight how our sales have increased—and there is nothing about it in here!"*

   You: *"You're right, I forgot to include sales statistics. I want to correct that. I'll have them to you by the end of the day."*

   Boss: *"These memos were filed all wrong."*

   You: *"I did that wrong? Wow, I didn't know that— thanks for telling me. How could I have done it better?"*

   Partner: *"If you want me to do something, don't yell at me."*

   You: *"You're right, it was inappropriate of me to yell. I apologize for that."*

   What to do:
   Agree immediately by uttering the two sweetest words in the English language: "You're right." Then go on and ask for help and guidance in straightening out the problem, or ask for suggestions for doing it right the next time. Learning something from the mistake gives the whole situation a redeeming significance that leaves you and everyone involved feeling much more positive.

GIVING CRITICISM

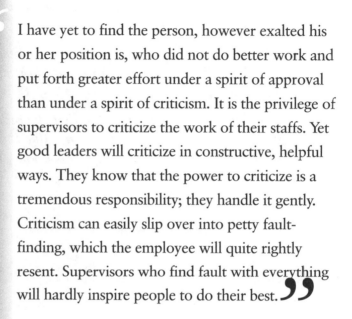

> I have yet to find the person, however exalted his or her position is, who did not do better work and put forth greater effort under a spirit of approval than under a spirit of criticism. It is the privilege of supervisors to criticize the work of their staffs. Yet good leaders will criticize in constructive, helpful ways. They know that the power to criticize is a tremendous responsibility; they handle it gently. Criticism can easily slip over into petty fault-finding, which the employee will quite rightly resent. Supervisors who find fault with everything will hardly inspire people to do their best.
>
> – Charles Schwab

The three-part "I" message is the ideal tool for delivering criticism. It ensures that you will be concise, constructive, and non-judgmental. Depending on the situation, you can use it alone or combine it with other assertive sentences.

For example:

"When you interrupted me three times during my presentation today, I felt irritated, because it got the conversation off track."

"When you're late with your monthly statistics, I feel frustrated, because it holds up my report to New York. Let's brainstorm some things to do that will guarantee you will get them to me on or before the 5th."

"When you don't take your cups and plates back to the kitchen, I feel taken for granted because I end up doing it so we don't run out of them. What can we work out so this doesn't keep happening?"

"Right. I wasn't pleased with how that worked out, either. I'd really appreciate your suggestions about how to turn this around."

"I know we agreed that I wouldn't let the bills get this high and I can see why you are angry. I've thought of a couple of things we can do to get this under control. Will you go over them with me?"

Guidelines for Giving Criticism at Work

1. Base your criticism on realistic performance standards, preferably written into the job description.

2. Address only the behavior that person can control.

3. Describe the behavior rather than judge it.
   Deliver "I" messages.

4. Focus on the problem (not the personality) and mutually discuss ways to solve it.

5. When appropriate, state what the consequences will be if performance does not improve.

6. Check to make sure you have been understood clearly. Request active listening.

Women in the Workplace

> " Good business manners are different from social manners because the situation is different. Unlike proper social life, business is naturally competitive, and its goal is to get things done rather than to spread charm. "
>
> – Miss Manners

Competition. Like it or not, my dears, that is what the workplace is about.

Competition externally and internally is the nature of organizations. That's not to say that cooperation can't exist alongside—it can and it does. However, it behooves all of us to acknowledge and accept that competition is an enduring aspect of the workplace. We don't have to like it, but we do have to deal with it.

"But where I work there *is* no competition," says perky Tammy, a recent graduate with a shiny new M.A., in one of my workshops. "I work with mostly women at a non-profit and there's really no competition to speak of." She beams and several of the other women, seasoned veterans of the workplace, roll their eyes. They know at a gut level, Tammy's got a lot to learn.

She will learn that while there is a great range in the competitive climate of organizations—from the mostly cooperative to the highly competitive flat-out "dog eat dog"—there is some intrinsic competition in all of them due to finite resources and the nature of human interaction. There are only so many resources, positions, and perks in any workplace, such as salary, budgets, desk/office space, choice assignments, support staff, software licenses, and time for decision-makers to okay the use of all these things. And employees, no matter how benign the group, will always at some level be competing for validation, approval of their ideas, and the acknowledgment and/or reimbursement for those ideas and their efforts.

As Ellen Goodman puts it, "Every culture devises the admissions tests into adulthood that most fit its adult values... The adult world is, after all, built on the shifting grounds of friendship and competition. The double message of this society and economy are to get along and get ahead... We rarely address the conflict between these goals... It is common in everyday life to work with our competitors and to compete with co-workers."[22]

Some competition in the workplace is common, to be expected for the reasons discussed above, and simply appears to be necessary evil. But things get out of hand and destructive when competition gets toxic. In order to identify these differences, let's make a distinction between common and toxic competition.

COMMON COMPETITION VS. TOXIC COMPETITION

Common competition can be a vehicle through which we reach our goals, do outstanding work, and earn substantial rewards. We do the kind of work that is needed to improve the company's products and bottom line in the hope that the savings will be passed on to us through increased compensation. Under common competition, good efforts are rewarded with good benefits, and the best efforts are rewarded with the best benefits. The best thinkers and producers get the largest pieces of the money allotted for raises, or they get intangible rewards like flex time, extra vacation days, or the company box seats to the hockey game. A side effect of this process is that employees do their best work, not just for the company but also for themselves and their own esteem. Certainly this is common knowledge regarding common competition.

But wait...

Our reasonable assumptions implicitly assume that success and competition are one and the same thing. We assume that competition is necessary for productivity, that it "builds character" and is an inevitable part of human interaction. We believe that without competition we would be condemned to mediocrity. But we are dead wrong. Each and every one of these reasonable assumptions has been refuted by solid research.

Exhaustive study on competition by author Alfie Kohn[23] posed this question: "Do we perform better when we are trying to beat others than when we are working with them or alone?" After thorough research and synthesis of hundreds of studies, the evidence was so overwhelming and consistently clear, the answer to the question was: "Almost never." There are some innovative companies who have succeeded in continuous development and refinement of products and services because they have taken the research to heart. In these groups, sometimes referred to as "skunk-works," individuals are rewarded for working together in new ways. Members are encouraged to cooperate and build on

one another's ideas and discouraged from engaging in one-upmanship and intra-group competitiveness.

As so dramatically demonstrated by the recent mind-boggling business scandals, competition—sometimes rabid competition—remains the norm in most American workplaces. We will eventually integrate more and more of our standard habits and operating procedures into our work lives, just as we have integrated ourselves there. Some women who have attained positions of power are already doing just that—modeling more cooperative, less competitive work styles and establishing more family-friendly policies such as flexible work schedules and child care.

But as of this writing, it is men (and the overall spirit of competition that accompanies their leadership styles) who are in most positions of power in most workplaces. So until our workplace utopia dawns, women will need to use self-respecting, effective ways to deal with competition and consciously initiate new and more cooperative ways to do business. At the same time, we need to strive for leadership positions so we can establish policies and procedures dedicated to equal treatment, equal pay, equal opportunity and other family friendly changes.

The most obvious form of toxic competition is when co-workers take it so seriously that they sabotage each other's work, usually through passive-aggressive tactics. It can be withholding important information needed for others to do their job well, or it can be as overt as "losing" a report on its way to the UPS office, or even by deleting files on another employee's computer! This sort of thing surfaces when employees are openly pitted against each other for one prize. It often happens when resources are truly scarce and organizations try to get the most work out of everyone while skimping on the rewards. In common competition, everyone gets some kind of raise, but the most effective employees get bigger raises. In toxic competition, only a select few get raises—or worse, all but the chosen few get insulting increases in pay.

Praise is also scant in toxic competition. Employees may

work toward not being insulted versus being praised. Toxic competition can often feed on negative second-hand information, such as your manager telling you about how your peer is doing such a bad job. There's the implication that you must do better than him, which can be difficult if you know that he is really good at his job. Setting an unnaturally high bar for employees is a form of toxicity as well.

The main thrust of my career in educational psychology and organizational communication has been to develop more cooperative, less competitive schools and workplaces. I've seen firsthand, and the research on groups has unequivocally shown, that excessive competitiveness is inherently destructive.

Certainly, there are highly aggressive people (some women, more men) who are comfortable with—some even invigorated by—excessively competitive environments. The vast majority of us are not. We are frustrated, wounded, and drained by them. Too many talented and productive people are burned out by long term contact with highly aggressive co-workers. Unfortunately, steamrollers who are top producers and skilled at publicizing their accomplishments are highly prized in many organizations. The true havoc they wreak is usually understood fully only after they have left—if then.

If you work in such an environment or even with one exceedingly aggressive person, realize you are exposed daily to a toxic influence. Practice and polish the skills and lessons of Civilized Assertiveness (you will learn more in this and the following chapters), and then remember to remain on guard and be totally mindful in their presence.

The lion and the lamb may lie down together, but the lamb isn't going to get much sleep.

– Woody Allen

WHY DO WOMEN HAVE SUCH PROBLEMS WITH COMPETITION?

Competitive environments, in many ways, violate our history as women. Recall the language style differences in male and female cultures discussed in Chapter 3. As adults, women need civilized assertiveness to handle tough situations and—better still—to turn them to our benefit. That is, we need to acknowledge and handle competition and conflict, doing so with grace and mutual respect. And a little humor does wonders so long as it's not at our own or someone else's expense. Do not, however, use your wit with highly traditional, stuffy men whom you know to be chauvinists. In the 1920s, F. Scott Fitzgerald observed, "there is a large class of men whose egotism can't endure humor in a woman." Unfortunately, many of us have found out firsthand this hasn't changed.

Given the realities of common competition and the fact that women sometimes have to cope with highly aggressive individuals, a primary goal must be to consciously complete the common competitive tasks that are necessary for parity and for a more integrative use of our talents in the workplace. The essential first step is taking our heads out of the sand and making ourselves aware of the competitive games that are played incessantly in our organizations, in our institutions, and in our personal lives. Second, we must take action. Unless we choose to become counter-aggressive and manipulative, this will require practicing new language tactics, strategies, and vocabularies to counter and defuse the more destructive aspects of the competitive model.

GAMESMANSHIP—A SPECIAL BRAND OF COMPETITION

It's a terrible irony that "they are not team players" is consistently at the top of the list when men are asked why they don't like working with women. Here we are, the virtuosos of compromise, harmony, and cooperation, and we're getting low scores for teamwork! How can this be?

For starters, let's go back to the playground. Men are

socialized from childhood to rely extensively on hierarchy, competition, and rules to shape and regulate their behavior. One of the primary testing grounds for these trappings of power is their childhood play with other males. Indeed, the role of play in a boy's socialization is so central that many boys grow into adulthood talking about life and work in terms of "the game."

Under the umbrella of this metaphor, they make regulations, call fouls, pick teams, sort winners and losers, and generally carry on in a manner that taught them dominance on the sporting field and in other forms of play. In the process, they come to view competition and conflict as natural, inevitable, and manageable. Running from a fight constitutes forfeiting the game, so most men learn to stand their ground, face the foe, and give it their best. While the boys were learning gamesmanship (faking plays, keeping "one-up," polishing their bravado), girls were being "nice" (taking turns, giving each other praise, encouragement, and compliments).

The pervasiveness of the game metaphor explains why men are so baffled when the women who end up on their teams don't seem to understand the plays, don't pay much attention to the rules of play, and don't worship the competition. They conclude that women aren't playing with the team, when the truth is that women aren't even in the game and may in fact not even realize that a game is going on. Even when women do realize they're on a team and in a game, they're so relieved to be on a "team" and be "one of the guys" that they may not even hear the scores being announced.

Now we need to take a peek at the guys' playbook. In any mixed-gender situation, we must recognize that we already belong to a team whether we've been issued a jersey or not. Chances are, the whistle has blown and the game is already under way. At least some and perhaps most of the other players already know the rules. Engagement is inevitable. When we opt to avoid engagement in a setting where others are engaged, we are going to appear weak, fearful, and powerless.

Consider the case of Megan, a VP at a mid-sized consulting company. She complains bitterly about her co-worker, Terry, whom she describes as lazy, manipulative, and highly political. Terry has been dragging his heels on a joint project. He challenges Megan's need for the statistics she requests, is late with the little work he does get to her, and generally costs Megan a good deal of time and energy. But Megan wants to avoid conflict. She shrinks from the prospect of the confrontation that might produce a change in Terry's behavior. She continues to promptly send Terry any material he asks for, fills him in on meetings he doesn't bother to attend, and has even covered up several of his more serious foul-ups.

Megan, Megan! You're ceding the field without even testing how far you can throw the ball. You are actually rewarding Terry for his self-centered behavior. To make things worse, you are making yourself look like his fool and his patsy. Continuing to go out of your way with a colleague who rarely or never returns the favor is counterproductive, self-diminishing, and seriously in violation of the principle of balance. You are avoiding conflict, to be sure, but you are paying a premium price.

CIVILIZING GAMESMANSHIP

Once they give the game a try, women often find they enjoy it. Take the case of Constance Worth, CEO of a major business, who demonstrated her deftness in her first encounter with the company's new owner. Walking into a meeting where Constance was the only woman, he turned to her and asked for a cup of coffee. Without missing a beat, she replied pleasantly, "I'll get you coffee if you'll Xerox these papers for me." She did not raise her voice or glower, nor did she fetch the coffee while burying her annoyance under a truckload of resentment. She simply held her ground and let her position be known. She was assertive and civilized.

Many women—Megan is an example—can't even imag-

ine such boldness. They may consider the whole concept of gamesmanship to be disagreeable and possibly dishonest. Unnerving as it may be, however, the game goes on and our status is likely to be determined by our performance whether or not we want to play. To hold our own, we need to be able to do several things. First, we must recognize and not be taken in by the predictable ploys game players use to keep themselves "one-up." (See Common Ploys on the next page.) Second, we need to know how to react to and handle these games. And third, when we want to skip the gamesmanship, we need strategies for sitting the game out without communicating weakness. We don't have to try and be one-up, but we do have to stay even.

Think of handling gamesters with something like the same tactics used in a martial arts class. A punch thrown at you is similar to a game being aimed in your direction. You have two options to avoid being hit. The first is to deflect the punch with a sweep of your forearm or use your opponent's momentum to tumble him past you. Using this option, you engage the blow only long enough to neutralize it. The second option is to simply step aside from the punch and then sweep around to face your opponent squarely. This proclaims that you are willing to face him, but you are not willing to fight with him. The same thing happens in facing down gamesters—you engage him only long enough to confront and defuse their game, or you sidestep the ploy entirely with words or behavior that don't allow room for the game to begin. Either way, you show others that you are aware of the game and choose not to play.

Beware of These Common Ploys

VERBAL ONE-UPMANSHIP
- Excessive interrupting
- Answering questions directed to someone else
- Humorously disparaging ideas/work of others
- Answering questions in an "expert" tone of voice
- Giving permission when none is needed

DEFENSIVE DUMBNESS
- Didn't think you would mind
- Didn't realize that was your decision
- Didn't know you wanted to attend
- Didn't realize you hadn't been notified

"FORGETTING"
- "Forgets" to pass on information
- "Forgets" to include you in meetings
- "Forgets" to respond to your request
- "Forgets" he promised to pick something up
- "Forgets" you asked him to stop a particular behavior

EXCLUSION
- Key decisions are made in an exclusive setting (club, golf course, etc.)
- Your presence is ignored
- You are not asked for your opinion
- You are not included in the conversation

It's important to remember that games teach men not only to compete in but also to share camaraderie through the plays and ploys. Games are used to make, test, and seal friendly relationships. A brilliant demonstration of this is comedian Jeff Foxworthy's routine demonstrating men's friendly teasing: "Bob, you old pervert! How are you?!" He goes on to explain that women do not greet each other in a similar way: "Women never say 'hi' by yelling, 'Betty, you fat pig! Great to see you!'"

Men will call each other names and throw little insults each other's way as a sign of friendship—the message is: "If you can take a joke from me, you've got a sense of humor about yourself and are confident enough to hang around me." They sometimes use these with women, not realizing that our communication style is attuned to supportive compliments: "You look great today," "You did great work on the Potter project," and so on. Remember that boy in second grade who would pull your hair, then run away? He probably had a crush on you, and this was his fledgling brand of intimacy!

You still need to decode the friendly game behavior and distinguish it from the negative gaming. Ask yourself, does the man in question have normal and respectful conversations with you as well as fire zingers and needle you? In addition, look at other physical and verbal cues before you assume that someone is trying to one-up you when they seem otherwise friendly. You may decide to just let some things go—noblesse oblige. But if something deeply bothers you, then you need to speak up. Confronting them about it in a pleasant way—preferably with a dose of humor—is the epitome of civilized assertiveness.

NOTES

The Ten Commandments

1 Thou shalt ask for what thou wants and needs.

2 Thou shalt not make self-diminishing or apologetic comments.

3 Thou shalt listen to other viewpoints with an open mind.

4 Thou shalt not be too swift with praise or agreement.

5 Thou shalt hold the line in discussions and decision-making on important issues.

6 Thou shalt not ask for personal permission or approval.

7 Thou shalt take credit for thy work and ideas.

8 Thou shalt make more assertions and ask fewer questions.

9 Thou shalt use neutral language rather than emotional language.

10 Thou shalt choose thy conflicts.

*T*his final chapter pulls together the skills, strategies, and techniques of civilized assertiveness and presents Ten Commandments for the workplace and beyond. Chisel them into your heart and mind.

Let's look more closely at each of these points and see how they play out at work.

1   Ask for what you want and need.

Examples:
"I need extra help to work on this project so we can complete it by Friday."
"I'm not comfortable with working late nights. However, I am willing to come in early each day—that's the time I'm sharpest."

Not knowing how to ask for what they want and need is the root problem for many of the women who have taken my workshop. In their eyes, coming out and saying what you want or need is "selfish and unfeminine." Quite the contrary, it makes you much easier to understand and talk to. In a recent class, Mandy, a competent, engaging woman in her early forties, fumed about being passed over for a promotion at work. When I asked what her boss had said when she asked to be considered for the job, her reply was, "Oh, I never said anything; it was evident that I was the best candidate for the position." Dear heavens, no, no nooo! Never assume that anything is ever evident to supervisors—or co-workers—or anyone, anywhere, for that matter. They are so preoccupied with their own tasks and lives that they don't have the energy to notice everything you do and are. Even on the off chance that a supervisor knows what you want, hearing you ask for it reaffirms what she knows and demonstrates that you have the confidence and savvy to go after it in a businesslike manner.

When asking for what you want from a co-worker or subordinate, it is vital that you be clear and direct. Civility and an even tone of voice are important, but directness and clarity are the key. As a young professor and director of the Learning Center at Regis University in Denver, I was assigned an administrative assistant considerably older than me. Hazel was of such great help to me—almost psychic—but I had the hardest time asking her for what I needed done. Her age and experience intimidated me, and I felt almost like I was insulting her by asking her to type something. One day while I hemmed and hawed, she finally burst out, "Judith, please! Just tell me what you want me to do for you—it's my job!" In that instant, I realized that by not being clear, I had been making both of our jobs a good deal harder to do.

Letting an office superior (notice I said just "office superior"—this person is not your superior as a person!) know what you want or need can be somewhat tricky. You will need to focus on carefully modulating your voice and using more tentative words in your request. You want to let her know what you need, but you don't want it to come out as a demand or a lecture.

Team Talk Troubles

Until the last 15 or 20 years, office structures were quite clear and personnel hierarchies were maintained. Generally, employees addressed their supervisors by "Mr.," "Miss", or "Mrs.," plus their last name. Most personnel considered their supervisors "bosses." Currently, many of even the most buttoned-down offices allow for a Casual Friday. Today's offices are frequently "open plan"—employees sit in open desks and cubicles near their bosses. Even the language has changed. "Bosses" are considered "managers" and insist on being referred to as team members, so "Mr. Swenson" becomes "Dave."

"Workers" are "teams" and in many workplaces, everyone became equal. You aren't just employees and employers—you are pals!

Right? Right, you're all equal—but some are more equal than others.

The "we're-all-buddies" concept breaks down quickly when things are not going well and there is increased stress. As soon as problems arise—imminent layoffs or dissension in the ranks—a manager is quite likely to pull rank. Your "manager" turns into a "boss" and makes uncharacteristically authoritarian comments or decisions. Joking and questioning his decisions are no longer tolerated. The truth is, it doesn't matter how "equal" your "manager" says the two of you are. If he decides your compensation and performance review and assigns your work, then he is your boss, plain and simple. Call him "Al" but think "Sir."

ASKING FOR WHAT YOU WANT FROM AN UNCLEAR SUPERVISOR

Pam's boss Anton drives her insane. He drops last-minute work on her and is frequently unclear about expectations or what the outcome or product of her work should be. Adding to the problem is his volatile nature. Under stress, he yells at her for even minor mistakes and in any instance when things haven't turned out well. After yet another last-minute project has been thrown at her, Pam is ready for some better directions and a little respect to boot.

Pam:	Anton, I appreciate your confidence in me to get things done. However, in order to get things done as well as possible, I believe I need more time to complete tasks.	*Positive statement* *"I" statement, clear and short*
Anton:	Oh, Pam, you're so good at what you do, time's NEVER an issue!	*Deflection with an overblown compliment*
Pam:	Thanks, but this is an issue for me. For example, that memo you handed me at 4:30 yesterday to be done and sent out by 5:00 required a fair amount of research to be done. Some of the info I needed couldn't be found in thirty minutes. And I realized this morning that one of the numbers I put in it was incorrect. I really think the project I sent out wasn't up	*Thanking Anton, then reestablishing that this is indeed a problem is a polite form of Broken Record* *Specific example of her complaint*

to my standards or our company's. So I really need more time to do it justice.

Anton: Well, sometimes things just have to be done fast.

Deflection with a statement of the obvious

Pam: Yes, they do. But I am uncomfortable with sending out incorrect work. I'd like more time to complete complicated jobs in order to do them well.

Responding to truth in statement

Framing the request in the service of the job

Anton: Well, look, that memo I asked you to do yesterday didn't have to be that precise. It just needed some average numbers and prices on it.

Deflection and hedging

Pam: Oh, I didn't get that impression. I certainly would have come up with some estimates rather than hunting down all those numbers if I had understood that.

Fogging

Rephrased "I" statement with effect of how his action helps her

When you give me assignments, can we sit down and go over what's involved so I can pace myself and get things done faster?

Anton: I thought I told you. Besides, you should know stuff like that.

Brush-off, insinuation that Pam is ignorant

| Pam: | Perhaps I should know things like that. But I didn't know, and I know how important it is to you to have all the facts straight when things go out. How about when you give me a new assignment, we sit down for just a few minutes and discuss the scope and deadline for it? | *Fogging*

Frames request as a benefit to him

Negotiation of a viable solution to benefit them both |

Pam's approach has a great chance of working for her because of her choice of words. She needs Anton to be clearer with her on assignments and to give her more time to complete them so she doesn't go crazy. However, by reframing the request in the service of the job, it "eases" the force of the request and highlights the benefits to Anton and the company. Pam knows from experience that Anton is unclear and can be disorganized, so her proposal to meet at the start of each assignment will solve her problem of getting unclear information and will only take a bit of Anton's time. While he may agree to this, Pam keeps the ball in her own court by being the one to remind Anton of the agreement and getting a moment to review the assignment.

When working with unorganized people, it is important to keep yourself super-organized; it helps you and makes you look very professional when others take notice of office dynamics. Now, Anton complying with Pam's request does help the company by producing quality work, but Pam's reframing of the request is reminiscent of Tom Cruise's line to Cuba Gooding Jr. in "Jerry Maguire": "Help me help you!" She also tones down her phrases: "I need…" and "I want…" become "It would be helpful if you could…" and "I'd like…" She uses these more relaxed demands to refocus Anton's lame deflections and to tie her requests together—all in the service of the job.

2 No self-diminishing or apologetic comments.

Nothing diminishes your message like a qualifier or tag that implies you're unsure of or unqualified to make this statement. Qualifiers are phrases like:

"I'm probably wrong about this, but..."

"This may seem silly, but..."

"I'm sorry, but..."

No, you're not sorry! Remember especially how useless the word "sorry" is. It and the rest of these qualifiers mark you as a person who doesn't even fully believe what she's about to say. If you're really that unsure about the statement, should it even be said? If an idea needs an apology, perhaps it shouldn't be brought up!

Tags are qualifiers that end a sentence. They look for reassurance from others that the idea or statement is okay. Some examples are:

"...don't you think?"

"...wouldn't you say?"

"...don't you?"

Perhaps they don't. But don't worry about someone else in the same sentence as your statement. If you really care, ask them in a separate and complete sentence: "I don't think he's ready to handle this project by himself. Do you feel differently?"

What if you catch yourself saying one of these powerless phrases? Stop mid-sentence, then continue with the actual statement. Reinforce what you really want to say.

"You might think this is...well, I don't know what you'll think, so here's my suggestion..."

"This could be really profitable, don't you think?...I certainly do."

3   Listen to others' viewpoints with an open mind.

This commandment can be best summed up in this quote from communication expert and cognitive psychologist George Miller:

In order to understand what another person is saying, you must assume that it is true and try to imagine what it could be true of.

The eloquence of this statement is that it gets to the core of active listening with great brevity. The process of actively listening to another's (frequently conflicting) viewpoint does one of two things for you. First, it can separate the wheat from the chaff by forcing the other person to explain his viewpoint so clearly that it either makes some sense or is obviously full of holes. Second, fully hearing the other person can give you an insight that you would not otherwise have had. Good ideas can come from anywhere and anyone, and you might find something useful in what the other person says even if you don't agree with the final outcome of his train of thought. Most importantly, good listening is respect made tangible. The other person gets that benefit, and in turn, by and large, will give it back to you. Everyone wins in the respect game!

Keeping an open mind is hardest when listening to criticism. According to sociologist Pepper Schwartz, studies show that bosses avoid giving criticism to women who take it too personally. "Rather than face your reaction," she says, "they decide over time not to say anything. But then you don't hear what you need to hear."

4   Hold back on the praise and agreement.

We women tend to praise and agree with others almost as a reflex. In low competition workplaces in which the bulk of the staff is female, this kind of ready affirmation-giving is generally okay. However, in most other work situations, such as moderate to highly competitive workplaces or where there are as many or more men as women, you will need to curb your enthusiasm. Quick affirmations go right to the head of many men, and it simply feeds into the woman-supporting-the-man concept we spoke about in Chapters 2 and 3. Don't play into it! When praise (especially really flowery compliments) gets used too freely with men in the workplace, a male employee can start to feel like he can get away with more than he can or should. Much of his experience with female co-workers and supervisors leads him to believe "She won't mind—after all, she likes me and thinks I do great work!" It is a wise supervisor who begins with mild praise and asks for more details. An important habit to develop is to keep the praise specific and avoid global personal comments.

Wrong: *"Hey, that's a great idea!"*

"Oh Roger, you're so funny!"

Right: *"Hmm, that has some potential. Can you tell us more about it?"*

"Ha ha ha, Roger! That's a great joke! Where did you hear it?"

5   Hold the line in discussions and important decision-
    making conversations.

Our inclinations and socialization as little girls into adulthood tells us to go along to get along. Yes, that's easy to do, and
yes, it's sometimes harder to stand up for what you believe is
right. Remember the discussion in Chapter 2, "Talking With
the Men in our Lives"? Who benefits if we have experience and
insight and don't share it? There are three important points to
remember in holding the line:

- Don't back down in the face of disagreement: "I can see
  how you could see that, but I'm still not willing to fudge
  the numbers for this project."

- Speak up when you are being ignored: "I have
  something to contribute to this discussion—has anyone
  considered the financial ramifications of this decision?"

- Don't allow misinformation to pass: "Actually, I've
  found not two—but five—different suppliers for this."

HOLDING THE LINE WITH A RELUCTANT CO-WORKER

Kim is managing a marketing project at her office. One
of her team members, Mike, keeps dragging his feet in getting
his work to her so that the final presentation can go out on
time. He gives excuses and puts up resistance to her professional demands. Kim has had enough of the excuses and poor
(if not nonexistent) work, and she's ready to confront him.

Kim: Mike, I need to talk to you
about something for a minute.
I've appreciated the work   *Positive note*
you've done on this project.
As you know, we need to get
this marketing project done by
next Tuesday, so I need your   *"I" statement, clearly*
part done by this Friday.   *stated*

Mike: Aw, you don't need my stuff   *Trying to brush her off*
done that soon. I'll have it
ready on Tuesday morning.

Kim: No (pause), I need your part   *"No" statement, start*
done by Friday afternoon.   *of Broken Record*
I'll need it done that early so
I can proofread it along with   *"I" statement with a*
everyone else's parts, and   *clear explanation of*
that gives us time to fix   *reason (Variation on*
errors and format everything.   *Three-part "I"*

Mike: It won't take that long to   *statement)*
check everything and print it!

Kim: It might not, Mike, but I'd   *Fogging*
rather have the time and not
use it than not have the time
and need it. So, I need your   *Broken Record*
part by Friday afternoon.

Mike: Well, um…I still haven't
gotten those figures from
Sherrie. You know how she is
with returning phone calls.

Kim: I'm sure she can be reached;   *Negotiation/*
she has e-mail and a fax   *Problem-solving*
number, too.

Mike: Well, I have faxed her and e-mailed her, and she won't call me back.

Kim: So you're saying that no matter what you do to contact her, you can't get her to respond to your requests.

Active listening

Mike: Yeah, totally!

Kim: O.K., at ten this morning, let's call her in a conference call and we'll get the answers we need.

Negotiation

Mike: Oh, that's all right, I'll just keep trying her.

Trying to brush her off again

Kim: That hasn't been working, Mike, and if this is what's holding you up in getting your part done by Friday, then let's do this together and help you get your stuff done, right?

Variation on "No" statement

Variation on Broken Record

Mike: (shrugging) Yeah, okay.

Kim: Good. After we call Sherrie, let's brainstorm a bit to make sure you have all you need to get your part done.

Negotiation

Kim's assertive approach and solution does several things. She has subtly let Mike know that she's on to him, and she's not letting him slack off anymore. With Broken Record, she's not letting him talk her out of her original request, as it is a reasonable

one. The first solution she negotiated will allow her (therefore Mike) to knock obstacles out of his way so he can finish his work on time. Calling Sherrie together will not only get the results he needs, but it will also either shed some light on Sherrie's habit of not calling Mike back or reveal if Mike has actually been that diligent in calling her. The second solution will clear up any remaining problems, leaving Mike no choice but to finish on time, or worse, face the fact that he just couldn't do his assigned tasks.

6   Don't ask others for personal permission or approval.

Here's a place where the importance of nuancing our language is evident. I'm referring to *personal* approval and affirmation, not *professional* approval of your work. The people with whom you work are not and cannot be responsible for telling you what a great person you are. Their only responsibility to you is to work with you and let you know how your job performance is going, how competent you are in your position. What you want and need from them is to help you catch mistakes in your work before it becomes official or leaves the office. You need them to look over your work and brainstorm solutions to any problems you or they find. What we need to know from co-workers and supervisors is, "Is this work acceptable?" (The only time this general question should be asked is during a yearly or quarterly performance review. Otherwise, frame your questions to a specific item or task in order to get focused feedback.) Remember, it's all in the service of the job.

Wrong: *"Okay, so I'll cover the Los Angeles project...?"*

"Does this report look okay?"

Right: *"I'll cover the Los Angeles project unless there are any objections."*

"Would you check this for factual and grammatical errors?"

7   Take credit for your work and ideas.

And there is a corollary to #7—you must confront those who try to steal or diminish your ideas.

Ah, the ploys of boys (and some girls, as well). Just when you thought you and everyone around you were grown-ups, here come more games—the kind that really hurt because they involve people trying to steal or insult your ideas or viewpoints. These sorts of games are perfect examples of toxic competition (p. 131).

You can tell when you're being had, by that tingling on the back of your neck, a churning in your stomach, or a sudden heat flash or flushing of your face. You might have told others about it: "I was so shocked, I didn't do anything!" "I thought of what to say ten minutes later in my car, of course!" "I couldn't believe it was happening!"

Well, my dear ladies, I trust I have provided sufficient evidence to make you believe it from here on out.

Assertiveness Alert!

PHYSICALLY	EMOTIONALLY
increased heart rate	resentful
palpitations	uncertain what to do
tension in neck/shoulders	trapped
dry mouth	angry
butterflies in stomach	bitter
sudden fatigue	used
	insulted

In order to stand up for ourselves in a civilized fashion, it is essential that we remain mindful. If we are on automatic pilot instead of on alert, chances are we will react foolishly.

There are several common responses to aggression and toxic competition—none of them pretty. We may cave in and become self-diminishing with mea culpas and apologies. We may become too nicey-nice and eager to please. Or conversely, we may push back in a counter-aggressive snit. Possibly we will become manipulative and deceptive. These reactions often make us feel guilty or embarrassed, and they most certainly diminish us in our own eyes and those of anyone observing.

Once you know the physical, mental, and emotional warning signs, you know it's time to stand up for yourself. And yes, you have to do it—because no one else is going to. The best part about standing up for yourself is that eventually, people get the picture: You can't be gamed, and you're a person to be taken seriously. When you confront the game-player, you can often diffuse the tension and situation through a few words. Game-players aren't used to being challenged by women. In a majority of cases, they either back down or their argument falls apart.

Examples:

> *"Why, Jim! I'm glad you ended up liking my idea. When I mentioned it to you the other day you didn't seem very enthusiastic about it. As I was telling Jim at the coffee bar, I think we should..."*

> *"I sense some disapproval in that statement, Alex. What concerns you about the results of my idea?"*

8 Make more statements and ask fewer questions.

Time for a quick quiz!

True or False: Asking questions is a good thing in the workplace.

True or False: Asking questions is a bad thing in the workplace.

The fact is both are true, depending on the situation. Some questions are good because they give us more information and allow us to do things right the first time. However, certain kinds of questions and their phrasing simply aren't helpful (see commandment #2). I often wonder if women realize how frequently they end their sentences with a questioning tone? Do they know? How annoying? That is? Asking lots of questions and turning statements into questions are signs of subordinate speech. The questioning tone denotes a lack of confidence, and that only hurts us. Using assertions and statements instead of questions will either elicit an affirmation of the decision or a correction of information. Sometimes you can use an assertion to break a stalemate or to make a decision in any discussion that keeps going around and around.

Wrong: *"When is this due? Are we using the old or new format for the presentation? Who will be working with me on this?"*

Right: *"When is this due? Good, I'll use the new presentation format for this, and I'll take two people from my staff to complete this, unless I hear otherwise."*

When you take yourself and your ideas seriously, others will eventually follow suit. Those who do not are usually the gameplayers who realize you can't be gamed. That small minority usually learns to avoid contact with you since the manipulation doesn't work. Meanwhile, the rest of our coworkers can benefit from you explanations while you clarify them for yourself. No, this commandment isn't easy, but it's one of the best things you can do for yourself.

9 Use neutral rather than emotional words.

A wise supervisor I know always tells his new young employees, "I ain't your mama and daddy." Truer words were never spoken! Work is to compensate you for your efforts and productivity, not to support your self-esteem and hold your hand (see commandment #6). The good news about this fact is that it's also not your job to do this for anyone else. It has been said that a well-run organization is a dull one, and there's a ring of truth to that—as well as a certain amount of comfort. You don't have to be good pals with your co-workers (or even like them) in order to get things done at work; you simply have to respect them—and they you. Lois Haber, a partner in a successful financial services company, recalls being so non-assertive that male executives at other firms often ignored her. She credits her partner with forcing her to claim her real power. "Once I was at a meeting at a bank and there were 10 or 15 people around a conference table. Every time I started to talk, the men would ignore what I was saying and talk over me. After the meeting, I said to my partner, 'Look, you know what they were doing. You saw. Why didn't you do something?' He said, 'Lois, you just have to learn to do that yourself. You just have to jump in.'"[24]

SUPERVISING AN IMMATURE EMPLOYEE

Karen has been having problems with her new administrative assistant, Tiffany. She isn't conscientious about her work. She does things late or at the last minute, and even after repeated training, incorrectly. She spends a lot of time chatting or surfing the Internet. She generally shows signs of immaturity. It's bothering everyone, including Karen's boss. Karen realizes that this needs to stop or the girl will lose her job, reflecting negatively on Karen herself!

Karen:	Hi, Tiffany. There's something I want to discuss with you. When's a good time for just you and me to talk?	
	(later)	
	I like how pleasant you are with clients when they come in. It really reinforces our company's emphasis on customer service. However, I don't know if you realize that much of the rest of your performance here leaves something to be desired.	*Positive statement* *Statement of problem*
Tiffany:	What?! But you just said you liked me and I was great!	*Taking things personally, out of proportion*
Karen:	Tiffany, I do like you, and your people skills are great, but we need to talk about some of your other job skills. For example, the filing that you do is still mixed up and incorrectly filed. Hasn't Janis shown you how we file orders versus filing test reports?	*Positive reinforcement* *Refocusing to behavior, not personality* *Specific example of the problem*
Tiffany:	Oh, Janis doesn't care how they're done, and besides, she's been having so many problems with her boyfriend lately I'm surprised she's making it to work! Yesterday, at the coffee bar, she said…	*Trying to change the subject and deflect the focus*

Karen: I'm really not concerned with Janis. I'm concerned with your work, Tiffany. When you file things incorrectly or don't get things done on time, I feel frustrated because I can't get my job done efficiently.

Refocusing discussion

Three-part "I" statement

Tiffany: (begins weeping) Oh no, now I'm screwing up everything! I can't do anything right!

More generalizing, taking things personally

Karen: Tiffany, you're not screwing everything up. Parts of your work performance need improvement. It's a change that I know you can make.

Refocusing discussion

Positive reinforcement

Tiffany: Look, I do my job WAY better than Janis, and she got a raise last year and I didn't! And I've been carrying all the slack since this boyfriend crisis of hers started almost a month ago!

Karen: It sounds like you've got some concerns about your workload.

Active listening

Tiffany: Well, duh! I do everything and Janis does nothing!

Karen: Well, Tiffany, that doesn't   *Refocusing discussion*
          change the fact that you've
          still got some
          improvements to make in
          your work. However, you   *Fogging*
          might have some valid
          concerns. How about we   *Negotiation*
          have a ten-minute meeting
          first thing each morning to
          keep your workload clear
          and manageable?

Tiffany's immaturity and emotional outbursts make this exchange very difficult. Karen keeps refocusing the discussion by returning to the job performance and not Tiffany herself; she is employing a form of Broken Record. She also has to keep a modulated tone of voice in speaking with Tiffany because of her sobs and personal angst. Karen's solution to have daily meetings about Tiffany's tasks does two things. First, Karen can find out what Tiffany has done, what she hopes to accomplish that day, and any problems she has encountered in the process. Karen can then monitor and guide her toward success in her job. Second, it allows Karen to document Tiffany's work and progress, which keeps a good, solid paper trail in case Tiffany's work doesn't improve and she has to be fired.

10 Choose your conflicts.

Just as you can choose not to be assertive, it is important to remember that you can choose your conflicts. It is equally vital to know that, despite all the competition and games in the workplace, confrontations rarely have to turn into a "battle." Instead, you can just sort out a situation through a neutral discussion, or mutually work on solving the dilemma. Confronting a situation while using your assertiveness skills (Listen, Limit, Assert, and Negotiate) and the commandments (especially #9) can ease and air out a situation for everyone involved. People like to know where they stand with others, and you relieve them by letting them know that. Neutralize a potential conflict by creating a climate for constructive work.

Sometimes, however, you really have to save your energy for another issue. When co-workers—and especially supervisors—are under stress, there's only so much you can do. For example, a co-worker is going through intense personal problems, or perhaps your boss is under pressure to get a big project. They are going to be short with you and others, or forget things you've told them or that they've told you. It's not an excuse, that's just how it is. In these cases, the person under stress is not going to be receptive to any confrontations about their behavior. This can be especially true of a supervisor (see "Team Talk" on page 144). So what do you do in these situations? Here are four ideas:

■   Keep a respectful tone and use non-accusatory words—
     no lecturing.

■   Frame the request in the service of the job.

   Example:
   "When you detail the scope of this project, I
   can get it done much faster and with fewer
   mistakes."

■ When the words or behavior are negative, address how they affect you.

> **Example:**
> "When you yell at me like that, it really discourages me."

■ Keep all conversation with the person to work topics, not personal topics. Be polite and respectful, but not over-friendly. If they introduce a casual conversation topic, feel free to indulge a bit, but not too much.

You may still get some verbal abuse thrown your way from co-workers under stress, but you can do damage control—stay organized and allow time for mistakes as well as limit your verbal and social contact with them. In time, the problems will dissipate.

NOTES

Closing Thoughts

Civilized Assertiveness works with a vast majority of people in your life, but there are some on whom it has little effect. When you are dealing with those who have a drug or alcohol problem, a serious mental illness, or who are physically abusive or violent, you may find that your civilized assertiveness skills are irrelevant. Don't give up using these skills, but know that they aren't enough. These people need help that you can't provide. You can support them in getting the help they need, but you cannot be that help.

You also may find that some relationships don't work anymore because you are assertive. Either you will have to work with the person and come to a new understanding in your relationship, or it may end. Don't fear this: If someone doesn't want you to be confident and strong, they only want half a person—that's no longer who you are. As my friend Quentin Crisp defined it, "Style is being yourself—but on purpose." The same can be said for assertiveness—we cannot let anyone limit who we are.

THREE ESSENTIAL CHARACTER TRAITS

COURAGE

"From a timid, shy girl I had become a woman of resolute character, who could no longer be frightened by the struggle with troubles," wrote Anna Dostoevsky in her diaries. Courage is a fundamental character trait necessary for maintaining Civilized Assertiveness. It takes emotional and moral courage to speak out on important issues which are denied or opposed by those around you. It takes courage to tell the truth when others remain silent. And it takes courage to be the ultimate judge of your own behavior. In addition to courage there are two other character traits—perseverance and generosity—that I consider essential to the task of being your civilized and assertive self, your truest self.

PERSEVERANCE

Perseverance in the face of resistance, criticism, and failure is vital to sharpening and integrating civilized assertiveness principles and skills. Continuing to practice standing up for yourself in a civilized manner after a defeat is as important as learning the skill in the first place. We win some and we lose some—and we must not take a loss to mean our skills have failed us. As I noted earlier, others may be resistant to our new-found voice and may try to shame or criticize us into to not using it. That is the very time to use our new skills to renegotiate a better understanding of the relationship.

GENEROSITY

To open-mindedly negotiate and compromise with others while keeping your ego in check and your integrity intact requires a generosity of spirit that is central to civilized assertiveness. It is what allows us to focus on the positive and give others the benefit of the doubt. It is the basis of respect, fairness, and kindness in our dealings with others. A generosity of spirit allows us to be, in the words of John Henry

Newman, "tender towards the bashful, gentle toward the distant, and merciful toward the absurd."

And finally, I believe that those of us who practice the principles and skills of civilized assertiveness are forming a new aristocracy, in the sense that E.M. Forster uses the word:

"Not an aristocracy of power,
based upon rank and influence,
but an aristocracy of the sensitive,
the considerate, and the plucky...
They are sensitive for others
as well as for themselves,
they are considerate without being fussy...
and they can take a joke."

NOTES

1. Anne Eisenberg, "It's all in the Voice," *Denver Rocky Mountain News,* Monday, 13 November 2000.

2. Rosalind Miles, *Who Cooked the Last Supper?: The Women's History of the World* (New York: Three Rivers Press 2001), 13.

3. Eleanor Maccoby, "Gender and Relationship: A Developmental Account," *American Psychologist,* 45 (1990): 513-520.

4. Margaret Atwood, *Cats Eye* (New York: First Anchor Books 1998), 110-11.

5. Suzette Elgin, *The Last Word on the Gentle Art of Verbal Self-Defense* (New York: Prentice Hall 1987), 17.

6. Linda Carli, "Gender Differences in Interaction Style and Influence," *Journal of Personality and Social Psychology,* 56 (1990): 565-577.

7. Linda Carli, "Gender, Interpersonal Power, and Social Influence," *Journal of Social Issues,* 55 (1999): 725-743.

8. The characteristics of the passive, aggressive, and assertive styles were culled from Chapter 3 in Madelyn Burley-Allen, *Managing Assertively: How to Improve Your People Skills* (New York: John Wiley 1983), 35-57.

9. St. Paul's epistle to Timothy, *1 Tim. 2:11-12.* Note that biblical scholars do not believe that the epistle was actually written by Paul but by an unknown author using Paul's name to give authority to his own pronouncements. See Jouette M. Bassler, Ph.D., *The HarperCollins Study Bible: New Revised Standard Version,* ed. Wayne A Meeks (New York: Harper Collins 1993), 2229.

10. Charles Contreras, Ph.D., *How to Fascinate Men* (Cleveland, Ohio: Chesterfield Publishing Company, 1953), 63.

11. John Gray, Ph.D. *Men are from Mars, Women are from Venus* (New York: Harper Collins, 1992), 145-146.

12. Cynthia B. Costello, Vanessa R. Wright and Anne J. Stone eds., *The American Woman 2003 -2004: Daughters of a Revolution—Young Women Today* (New York: Palgrave McMillan, 2003), 76-77.

13. Beverly Byrum, "The Nuts and Bolts of Assertiveness Training," *University Associates Annual* (1988), 150.

14. Adapted from the comprehensive lists in Burley-Allen, *Managing Assertively,* 35–57.

15. Byrum, "Assertiveness Training," 149.

16. The concept of mindfulness is fully developed in Ellen J. Langer, *Mindfulness* (Reading, MA: Addison-Wesley, 1990).

17. James J. Lynch, MD, *The Language of the Heart: The Body's Response to Human Dialogue* (New York: Basic Books, 1985).

18. Manuel Smith, *When I Say No I feel Guilty* (New York: Bantam Books, 1975), 74.

19. Thomas Gordon, Ph.D. and Linda Evans, "Effectiveness Training for Women." (Washington, DC: *Psychology Today Tapes,* 1983).

20. I have added the sixth item to the original list of five found in Robert Bolton, Ph.D., *People Skills* (New York: Touchstone Press, 1986), 146.

21. Adapted from Burley-Allen *Managing Assertively,* 148-50.

22. Ellen Goodman, *Making Sense* (New York: Atlantic Monthly Press: 1989), 124.

23. Alfie Kohn, *No Contest: The Case Against Competition* (Boston: Houghton Mifflin Company, 1986).

24. Diane E. Lewis, "A Boardroom of One's Own," *The Boston Globe,* Friday, 17 April 1998.

BIBLIOGRAPHY

Alberti, Robert, Ph.D. and Michael Emmons, Ph.D. *Your Perfect Right*. San Luis Obispo: Impact Publishers, 1995.

Atwood, Margaret. *Cats Eye*. New York: First Anchor Books, 1998.

Barnett, Rosalind, Lois Biener and Grace Baruch. *Gender & Stress*. New York: The Free Press, 1987.

Bassler, Jouette M., Ph.D. *The HarperCollins Study Bible: New Revised Standard Version*. ed. Wayne A Meeks. New York: Harper Collins, 1993.

Bolton, Robert, Ph.D. *People Skills*. New York: Touchstone Press, 1986.

Bower, Sharon and Gordon Bower, Ph.D. *Asserting Yourself: A Practical Guide for Positive Change*. Reading, MA: Addison-Wesley, 1994.

Bramson, Robert. *Coping With Difficult People in Business and in Life*. New York: Ballantine, 1981.

Burley-Allen, Madelyn. *Managing Assertively: How to Improve Your People Skills*. New York: John Wiley, 1983.

Butler, Pamela, Ph.D. *Self-Assertion for Women*. New York: Harper Collins, 1992.

Byrum, Beverly. "The Nuts and Bolts of Assertiveness Training." *University Associates Annual* (1988), 150.

Carli, Linda. "Gender Differences in Interaction Style and Influence." *Journal of Personality and Social Psychology* 56 (1990): 565-577.

Carli, Linda. "Gender, Interpersonal Power, and Social Influence." *Journal of Social Issues,* 55 (1999): 725-743.

Coloroso, Barbara. *The Bully, the Bullied, and the Bystander*. New York: Harper Collins, 2002.

Contreras, Charles, Ph.D. *How to Fascinate Men*. Cleveland, Ohio: Chesterfield Publishing Company, 1953.

Costello, Cynthia B, Vanessa R. Wright and Anne J. Stone eds., *The American Woman 2003 -2004: Daughters of a Revolution—Young Women Today*. New York: Palgrave McMillan, 2003.

Crisp, Quentin and Donald Carroll. *Doing it With Style*. New York: Franklin Watt, 1981.

Dale, Paulette, Ph.D. *Did You Say Something Susan? How Women Can Gain Confidence with Assertive Communication*. Secaucus, N.J.: Carol Publishing Group, 1999.

Eisenberg, Anne. "It's all in the Voice." *Denver Rocky Mountain News*, Monday, 13 November 2000.

Elgin, Suzette. *The Last Word on the Gentle Art of Verbal Self-Defense*. New York: Prentice Hall Press, 1987.

_____ *Success, With the Gentle Art of Verbal Self-Defense*. New York: Prentice Hall Press, 1989.

Fitzgerald, F. Scott. "The Rich Boy" in *Babylon Revisited and Other Stories*. New York: Scribner Paperback Fiction Edition, 1996.

Gilligan, Carol, Ph.D. *In A Different Voice*. Cambridge: Harvard University Press, 1993.

Gordon, Thomas, PhD. *Leader Effectiveness Training: The No-Lose Way to Release the Productive Potential of People*. New York:Wyden Books, 1977.

Gordon, Thomas and Linda Evans. "Effectiveness Training for Women." Washington, D.C. *Psychology Today Tapes*, 1983.

Goodman, Ellen. *Making Sense*. New York: Atlantic Monthly Press, 1989.

Gray, John, Ph.D. *Men are from Mars, Women are from Venus*. New York: Harper Collins, 1992.

Harragan, Betty. *Games Mother Never Taught You*. New York: Warner Book, 1977.

Helgesen, Sally. Everyday Revolutionaries: *Working Women and the Transformation of American Life*. New York: Doubleday, 1998.

Jamieson, Kathleen Hall. *Beyond The Double Bind: Women and Leadership*. New York: Oxford University Press, 1995.

Kohn, Alfie. *No Contest: The Case Against Competition*. Boston: Houghton Mifflin, 1986.

Kohn, Alfie. *The Brighter Side of Human Nature: Altruism & Empathy in Everyday Life*. New York: Basic Books, 1990.

Lakoff, Robin. *Talking Power: The Politics of Language*. New York: Basic Books, 1990.

Langer, Ellen J. *Mindfulness*. Reading, MA: Addison-Wesley, 1990.

_____. *The Power of Mindful Learning*. New York: Perseus Publishing, 1998.

Lewis, Diane E. "A Boardroom of One's Own." *The Boston Globe*. Friday, April 12, 1998.

Lynch, James J, MD. *The Language of the Heart: The Body's Response to Human Dialogue*. New York: Basic Books, 1985.

Maccoby, Eleanor. "Gender and Relationship: A Developmental Account." *American Psychologist* 45 (1990): 513-520.

_____. "Perspectives on Gender Development." *International Journal of Behavior Development* 24 (4): 398-406.

Martin, Judith. *Miss Manners' Basic Training*. New York: Crown Publishing, 1997.

_____. Miss Manners, *A Citizen's Guide to Civility*. New York: Three Rivers Press, 1999.

Miles, Rosalind. *Who Cooked the Last Supper?: The Women's History of the World*. New York: Three Rivers Press, 2001.

Miller, George A. *The Psychology of Communication*. New York: Basic Books, 1975.

Montagu, Ashley. *The Natural Superiority of Women*. New York: Collier Books, 1952.

Pachter, Barbara and Susan Magee. *The Power of Positive Confrontation*. New York: Marlowe, 2000.

Phelps, Stanlee and Nancy Austin. *The Assertive Woman: A New Look*. San Luis Obispo, California: Impact Publishers, 1997.

Rubin, Jeffrey and Carol Rubin. *When Families Fight: How to Handle Conflict with Those You Love*. New York: Morrow, 1989.

Schaef, Anne Wilson, Ph.D. *Women's Reality*. New York: Harper Collins, 1992.

Shem, Samuel. MD and Janet Surrey, Ph.D. *We Have To Talk: Healing Dialogues Between Women and Men*. New York: Basic Books, 1998.

Smith, Manuel. *When I Say No I Feel Guilty*. New York: Bantam Books, 1975.

Tannen, Deborah, Ph.D. *You Just Don't Understand*. New York: Morrow, 1990.

_____*Talking From 9 To 5: How Women's and Men's Conversational Styles Affect Who Gets Heard, Who Gets Credit, And What Gets Done At Work*. New York: Morrow, 1994.

_____*The Argument Culture: Stopping the War of Words*. New York: Ballantine, 1998.

The American Woman 2003-2004: Daughters of a Revolution—Young Women Today. eds. Cynthia B Costello, Vanessa R. Wright and Anne J. Stone. New York: MacMillan, Palgrave, 2003.

Travis, Carol. *Anger: The Misunderstood Emotion*. New York: Touchstone, 1989.

White, Kate. *Good Girls Don't Get Ahead, But Gutsy Why Girls Do. Nine Secrets Every Career Woman Must Know*. New York: Time Warner, 1995.

Wollstonecraft, Mary. *A Vindication of the Rights of Woman*. G.B: Guernsey Press, 1995. Edited from the second revised edition, published in London in 1792 by Joseph Johnson.

Young, Cathy. *Ceasefire! Why Women and Men Must Join Forces to Achieve True Equality*. New York: Free Press, 1999.

Judith Selee McClure, Ph.D. is a business consultant specializing in interpersonal communication. As an educational psychologist, she was awarded the title of Professor Alumna following a distinguished teaching career at Regis University. She is president of Judith McClure and Associates, a company focusing on issues of communication, power and leadership. Her company provides training to numerous businesses including Raytheon, IBM and AT&T as well as nonprofit, state, and federal organizations.

Judith is co-author of *The Household Curriculum*. She received the Rocky Mountain Merit Award from the Colorado Council on Working Women for her contributions and commitment toward improving conditions for women. She conducts popular workshops based on the concepts of Civilized Assertiveness and lives in Denver with her husband.

For more information about Civilized Assertiveness, please visit www.civilizedassertiveness.com.

Additional copies of
Civilized Assertiveness for Women
can be ordered by sending a check or money order for
$17.95 plus $2.50 S&H to

Albion Street Press
2111 East Alameda Avenue
Denver, CO 80209-2710

or order online at
www.civilizedassertiveness.com